No Hiding Place: Child Sex Tourism and the Role of Extraterritorial Legislation

Jeremy Seabrook

Zed Books

LONDON • NEW YORK

in association with

ECPAT Europe Law Enforcement Group
AMSTERDAM

No Hiding Place: Child Sex Tourism and the Role of Extraterritorial Legislation was first published by Zed Books Ltd, 7 Cynthia Street, London N1 9JF, UK and Room 400, 175 Fifth Avenue, New York, NY 10010, USA in 2000 in association with:

ECPAT Europe Law Enforcement Group (End Child Prostitution, Child Pornography and Trafficking in Children for Sexual Purposes), legally represented by Defence for Children International (Netherlands Section), PO Box 75297, 1070 AG Amsterdam, Netherlands: e-mail: dcinl@wxs.nl; contact person: Annemieke Wolthuis.

Distributed in the USA exclusively by St Martin's Press, Inc., 175 Fifth Avenue, New York, NY 10010, USA.

Financial support from the European Union (EU) STOP Programme, the Dutch Ministry of Justice and Kindernothilfe in Germany for the original research, preparation and dissemination of the report *Extraterritorial Legislation as a Tool to Combat Sexual Exploitation of Children*, which provided the factual information contained in the book, is gratefully acknowledged.

Cover designed by Andrew Corbett
Set in Monotype Ehrhardt and Franklin Gothic by Ewan Smith, London
Printed and bound in the United Kingdom by Biddles Ltd, Guildford and King's Lynn

A catalogue record for this book is available from the British Library

Library of Congress Cataloging-in-Publication Data available

ISBN 1 85649 913 8 cased
ISBN 1 85649 914 6 limp

Contents

Acknowledgements

We would like to thank all those who contributed to the original study: Nadine Benichou, Regina Kalthegener, Ute Kreckel, Stan Meuwese, Muireann O'Briain, Ursula Schaffner, Regula Turtschi, Sophie Wirtz, Annemieke Wolthuis, Josephine Adauktusson, Elizabeth Martyn, Wanchai Roujanavong, Sudarat Sereewat, Toshiko Maya Sonozaki, Setsuko Tsuboi, Aron Tampoe.

Foreword

Poor children sexually abused by foreign visitors to their countries. What can be done about it?

In different parts of the world, children are the victims of a growing phenomenon: child sex tourism. Every child in every part of the world is entitled to a childhood, and to protection from sexual abuse. ECPAT investigated what can be done to improve legal and other procedures in combating child sex tourism.

The case studies that gave rise to this book examined the operation of a complex legal issue, namely extraterritorial jurisdiction. The ECPAT Europe Law Enforcement Group wanted to show how child sex offenders had been and could be prosecuted in their own countries, if they had managed to escape the jurisdiction in which they had committed the offence. We also wanted to get a better understanding of this 'tool' of international law, and to share that understanding with those responsible for the implementation of child protection laws. In this way the 'tool' could be used more frequently and to better effect.

But we were a small group of lawyers and technical experts. And because we concentrated on the legal issues, our work was somewhat indigestible for the general public. Yet we felt that the public would be interested in these cases and in the issues they raise. How does a prosecutor in one country get the information about an offence against a child in another country when he does not speak the language of that country? How is a complaint by the child sex assault victim followed up if the crime was committed by a foreigner? What kind of person pursues foreign children for sex? What are developing countries doing about such cases? It was in order to make the case studies accessible to a wider public that this book was written.

We are very grateful to Jeremy Seabrook, the author, who has not only brought the cases to life, but has also added his personal reflections on child sex tourism. In this publication we, as travellers and consumers, are driven to re-evaluate our notions of child protection and our responsibilities towards children in a world of consumerism and huge differences in economic power.

The book also invites us to understand the ways in which our institutions of state operate, or fail to operate, to fulfil their obligations to the world's children. The priorities they choose will depend on what the public wants to support. In ECPAT International we have campaigned for better law enforcement to protect all children, whatever their nationality, against sexual exploitation. We hope that you, having read this book, will find reason to support this aim.

Muireann O'Briain, S.C.
Executive Director, ECPAT International

Introduction

Many Western countries, as well as Japan, have recently enacted legislation that allows the arrest and trial of their nationals at home for offences committed against children in other countries. This has been in response to growing concern over privileged males (a majority of whom are from the West) who visit Third World countries for the purpose of sexually abusing children. Until the early 1990s, there was little that could be done to pursue such offenders once they had returned to their countries of origin. In any case, their presence in Third World countries that were opening up to tourism was not obviously harmful – they had gone as bona fide travellers, and often posed as benefactors, even 'rescuers', of the children of poor families. The authorities in the countries they visited, including those where legislation against child abuse was explicit, were often reluctant to pursue them, even when stories of their activities began to circulate. The foreign exchange they brought to impoverished regions of the world seems to have earned them a certain shield against scrutiny. Police were often more concerned with easier targets – petty infringements of the law by the poor, the taking of money from small traders in return for allowing them to pursue their lawful occupation. There was also a marked tendency to blame the victims, even when these were children, and to criminalize them as 'prostitutes' or 'street-children'. Corruption, too, allowed many offenders to get away with it – the authorities could sometimes be bought off by what, to well-to-do Westerners, was a small sum. The whole problem was concealed to some degree by the more widespread, legal and highly lucrative sex trade.

That this changed so quickly during the 1990s is due in large measure to the work of a number of non-governmental organizations (NGOs) in the countries that had become the destination of child-abusers. These established a network of sympathizers in the West. Together, they brought considerable pressure to bear on Western governments. By judicious use of the media they raised the profile of an issue that had previously been seen – where it had been acknowledged at all – as only a marginal problem, affecting a few rare individuals.

ECPAT (End Child Prostitution in Asian Tourism, later broadened to End Child Prostitution, Child Pornography and Trafficking in Children for Sexual Purposes) was one of the principal actors in this process. It soon became clear that in most countries, the NGOs were pushing at an open door. The stories emerging in the Western countries themselves about child abuse – within families and neighbourhoods, in children's homes, in state agencies established for the protection of children – nourished a growing public revulsion against such crimes. At times the strength of feeling became so overwhelming that a more general atmosphere of suspicion and distrust began to surround almost anyone working with children. However that may be, it became clear in the early 1990s that what was not tolerated at home should not be permitted abroad. It was perceived as hypocrisy that offenders should be pursued with the utmost rigour for what they did in their own country, while when they were abroad they could do as they chose with some of the most defenceless and vulnerable children on earth.

ECPAT and others working in the field make a distinction between the 'circumstantial' and the 'preferential' offender. The first term refers to people who will have sexual relations with an under-age person if the opportunity presents itself, but who will not necessarily seek out such partners. The preferential offender means one whose desires are explicitly focused upon children or those at or around the age of puberty. This is an important distinction, since the former may well be deterred from offending by campaigns against child sex tourism, while the latter are more likely to pursue their objectives in spite of the obstacles in their path. Of the cases in the book, the majority must be classified as preferential, although some of the individuals – perhaps Thierry and Boonen – may be seen to fall into the opportunistic category.

Extraterritorial legislation already existed to cover certain offences, notably international agreements on terrorism, narcotics, arms-dealing and other serious crimes. The proposal to arrest, try, and punish Western nationals in their own countries for sexual offences against children committed elsewhere in the world marked a new departure from extradition treaties and transnational cooperation in the pursuit of justice.

This book records the speed and efficiency with which this initiative was accomplished, as well as the impediments and difficulties in obtaining the necessary degree of collaboration between governments and authorities from quite different judicial traditions, values and cultures. The successes recorded here are once more a tribute to the tenacity and persistence of NGOs; the failures show how much more work remains to be done.

Sex tourism is itself a consequence of globalization, of the ease with which privileged people can now move around the world. This facility is not, of course, extended to the poor. Quite the contrary. The prohibition upon the free movement of poor people, in contrast to goods and money, should not be ignored in this context. The efforts by Europe to exclude those now stigmatized as 'economic migrants' compels a majority of the poor of the earth, victims of growing global inequality, to remain in their home countries. Whatever remedies for their poverty and desperation are proposed, moving to the West is not one of them. This sometimes leads them to sell their bodies, and occasionally even the bodies of their children. The expansion of travel and vacations, journeys and holidays have made tourism the largest single industry on earth. It is inevitable that among the vast number of people travelling to the Third World, some will go with purposes less honourable than the pleasure of travelling. In the mid-1990s, when about six million people visited Thailand annually, almost two-thirds of these were single males. Among them, it is only to be expected that some were attracted by the relative ease with which under-age young people might be procured for sexual purposes. In Thailand in 1995 I met a Frenchman who had employed a middle-aged woman as housekeeper in Thailand, while her niece – a girl of about 13 – shared his bed. This arrangement lasted until the aunt demanded more money than the Frenchman could pay. When she threatened to denounce him to the authorities, he pointed out that she would also be at risk in any investigation that followed. A 'settlement' was reached, and he paid off the aunt and the niece.

This example demonstrates another of the difficulties in pursuing such offences. Collusion between the 'guardians' of children and their abusers, often cemented by some monetary payment, serves as a powerful impulse to concealment. In extreme cases, relatives have sold their children to men who want to use them sexually. Among the stories in this book, there are at least two such examples: the van Engstraat and Langenscheidt cases, both in the Philippines.

These issues emerge in the case histories, as do the frequent misunderstandings, not only between Western sex tourists and their victims, but, equally, between officials and functionaries of differing cutural traditions and values. Some of the offenders have tried to use such differences to their advantage, declaring that their behaviour is sanctioned by the cultural practices, if not by the law, of the countries they visit. Certain cultural differences are real, but these cannot be used by offenders as an excuse for what they do. They are being pursued under the law of their own country, and they cannot be permitted to invoke the cultural practices of other countries to justify their activities.

Yet these cultural differences have to be addressed if effective co-operation is to be established between officials and law enforcement personnel coming from a variety of traditions. The whole question of what is a child – one that we may think beyond dispute – is actually a sensitive and contentious issue. The definition established by the United Nations Convention on the Rights of the Child – 'a child means every human being below the age of eighteen years' – is a useful guideline, but custom and culture in different parts of the world are unlikely to modify the habits of centuries overnight to comply with this view. This is reflected in the variation in the age of consent from country to country – in Japan it is as young as 13. When the children of the poor are expected to work for a living, to contribute to the maintenance of their families, it is only a short step to the perception of them as adults. That some such children will become sex workers, partly in response to a demand by relatively wealthy Western sex tourists, is not surprising.

Many other questions are raised by the cases in this study. One is the role of NGOs in the detection and pursuit of offenders, which fall more properly within the competence of the police and authorities of the country where the offence is comitted. The variations in the legal arrangements from country to country, the greater or lesser degree of severity with which some countries view the abuse of children – all these elements make cooperation between countries extremely difficult. Once again, the persistence of some of the principal actors has been a major feature of the relative success of the 15 cases that figure in this book.

Much may be learned from the ways in which the stories here came under public scrutiny. The deficiencies and strengths of each one serve as a guide for future action. The need for greater coordination between the agencies involved within a country, as well as between countries, becomes clear. How this may best be achieved is set out in the Recommendations.

The book is intended for all concerned with the protection of children, wherever they may be. Although the questions it raises have significant implications for international law, this is not the only purpose of the book. It is also intended to indicate how new forms of international cooperation in an increasingly integrated world may be possible, and to highlight issues that arise between growing gulfs of inequality in the global economy, one of the greatest being that between privileged Western men and the most neglected and abandoned children in the Third World.

The purpose of describing these case histories is not only to clarify the context in which they occurred, but also to bring them to the notice of all interested parties, including teachers and social workers, police and law enforcement personnel, those whose concern is with relations between rich and poor countries at the level of both governments and non-governmental agencies, and those involved in the development process itself.

Other questions emerge from the stories in this study. One of these is the relationship between the punishment of a few individuals who have injured children and the more intractable issue of social injustice. Legislation that facilitates the pursuit of abusers of children is no substitute for the wider responsibilities of what is increasingly called the 'international community' in addressing growing inequality between rich and poor, which itself helps to create the opportunities for the crimes depicted here.

A second question concerns the distinction between making an example of offenders against children and care for the children themselves. It is one thing to advertise to the world that this is behaviour that Europe will not tolerate, but another to ensure the well-being of the victims themselves. It seems that in these early cases there has been an eagerness to test the legislation, to measure its effectiveness in pursuing those who molest children; the fate of the children appears to be a lesser concern. This must be addressed if the legislation is to be taken seriously as a weapon in the armoury of child protection, as well as making answerable for their actions those who hitherto have abused children with relative impunity.

It is clear that some countries have pursued offenders with greater vigour than others. At the moment, there is only a single example from the UK, and none from the USA.

Child abuse is a highly charged question, so repelling that it often defies rational discussion. Those who have damaged children often have to be protected, both from public expressions of outrage, and when they are in prison. The emotions provoked by attacks on children reveal a great deal about the sensibility and psyche of societies. All this must be borne in mind when considering the effect of the blunt instrument that is the law in approaching the crimes set out in the stories that follow.

It is impossible to detach these from the atmosphere of rage and outrage that has surrounded discussion of child abuse in the West in recent years. It is not the intention of this book to contribute to the sense of hysteria and unreason that have clouded debate. In the United Kingdom in the early 1990s, a series of cases involving 'Satanic' rites around the abuse of children were apparently uncovered, and although the panic that this created was found to be largely unjustified, there nevertheless remains an element of the witch-hunt in the pursuit of those who commit offences against children. It is important to retain a perspective, and the impersonality of the law helps in this.

Extraterritorial legislation is a powerful instrument for curbing the activities of child-abusers who go to poor countries to take advantage of the most defenceless, but it will not of itself 'cure' the problem. It can be only one important element in a broader strategy, which must ultimately include confronting the issue of the great inequalities in wealth and power between abusers and their victims. If little can be done to reduce the inequality between adult and child that makes individual crimes unacceptable, the same fatalism should not operate when it comes to diminishing the great gulfs of social and economic inequality that are a significant factor in creating the opportunities for the offences described in this book.

No doubt, given the conspicuous profile the issue has assumed in recent years, and the fact that offenders come from all the rich countries, it is only a question of time before more examples from the United Kingdom and the United States appear in the growing body of sucessful prosecutions. But that is for the future. At present, with all their flaws, those described here have been pioneering cases.

Jeremy Seabrook

Introducing the Case Histories

The people of Europe must take responsibility for making sure that our nationals do not escape punishment simply by leaving the country where offences against children have taken place. Most European countries have now recognized that concerted international action is required to combat child sex tourism and the commercial sexual exploitation of children. They have enacted or extended existing extraterritorial legislation to cover the sexual abuse of children abroad. This has already been applied in a number of cases, and there is a growing jurisprudence in this area, both in Europe and in the wider world.

The very novelty of this legislation has led to a number of difficulties in practice. In some cases, the validity of evidence has been questioned. In others, the child victims have been treated insensitively. In yet others, there has been confusion over the role played by different participants in the process – Embassies, law enforcement agencies, prosecutors, NGOs, and so on. Some of these obstacles arise as a result of problems in communication between countries, different cultural attitudes, the varying requirements of legal systems, and the vigour with which the law is applied. Inadequate resources and the capacity of law enforcement personnel can also influence the outcome of a case. The deficiencies that have emerged demonstrate that there is a need to:

- analyse present mechanisms and procedures in the prosecution of cases of child abuse where extraterritorial jurisdiction has been applied;
- make available as widely as possible the information gained from existing cases; and
- develop guidelines, codes of practice and new procedures in co-operation, in order to help law enforcement authorities prosecute cases where more than one jurisdiction is involved.

The ECPAT Europe Law Enforcement Group

ECPAT International, with headquarters in Bangkok, comprises about 44 organizations worldwide, whose objective is to campaign against child prostitution, child pornography and trafficking in children for sexual purposes. ECPAT Europe is an informal grouping of European member organizations, within which the Law Enforcement Group was set up to promote more effective legislation and law enforcement for the protection of children against sexual exploitation. Funding was received from, among other sources, the European Union for research into the application of extraterritorial legislation in pursuit of child sexual offences. This book is a result of that work.

Origins of the Study on Extraterritorial Legislation

In all the ECPAT campaigns for better child protection, a recurring theme has been the necessity for developed countries to take responsibility for the actions of their nationals abroad. As a result of this, several countries have changed their laws, so that they may prosecute their nationals for offences committed against children abroad. Twenty countries now have such laws – Australia, Austria, Belgium, Canada, Denmark, Finland, France, Germany, Ireland, Italy, Japan, the Netherlands, New Zealand, Norway, Spain, Sweden, Switzerland, Thailand, the United Kingdom and the United States.

This is in line with recommendations made in the UN Convention on the Rights of the Child in 1989, the Committee of Ministers of the Council of Europe, and the Agenda for Action of the Stockholm World Congress against the Sexual Exploitation of Children in 1996. In 1996, the General Assembly of ICPO–Interpol endorsed the amendment of national laws for the same purpose, and in 1997, the Council of the European Union adopted a Joint Action Programme, which laid down measures for member states to review existing law and practice to ensure that their authorities can deal competently with the sexual exploitation of children.

Prosecution in a country where the offence was not actually committed presents many technical difficulties. To ensure a successful prosecution, close cooperation between the jurisdictions involved is vital. It is the objective of this study to analyse a number of cases to discover how effective the legislation is in practice. The aims of the study of the 15 case studies presented here are:

- to assess the effectiveness of extraterritorial legislation in fighting the sexual abuse of children;
- to provide examples of successful prosecutions for study by legislators, law enforcement personnel and child-protection NGOs;
- to identify problems, legal, technical or practical, in applying such legislation, and to make recommendations to improve strategies for the future;
- to clarify the roles of the main actors involved in such international prosecutions;
- to assess the advantages and disadvantages of different types of legal system in the application of such legislation; and
- to assess whether those countries that have recently enacted extra-territorial legislation encountered more difficulties in applying it than those in which it already existed.

Methodology

A questionnaire was submitted to those who reported on the cases chosen for study. Most of the case studies were undertaken by lawyers. The questionnaire sought *factual information* (how the case started, profiles of offenders and victims); information on *legal aspects of the case* (procedure, the steps taken in the different jurisdictions, the evidence available, the status of the victim before the court, whether the public interest was represented, the legal impact of the case, the role of the police); *social aspects* (the role of the media, the role of NGOs and of society in general); and finally, *miscellaneous aspects* (such as costs of investigation and prosecution).

Of the 15 cases, offenders came from Switzerland (4), the Netherlands (3), Belgium (2), France (2), Australia, Germany, Japan and Sweden (one each). The offences had been committed in Cambodia, the Czech Republic, the Philippines, Romania, Sri Lanka and Thailand. The cases are limited to those areas of the world from which information is available.

Some cases exemplify failure, since either there was no prosecution or there was an acquittal. It is important to stress that the focus is not on the personality of the offenders or the victims. Of the 15 cases, a conviction was obtained in 12, although some offenders have yet to serve a sentence. Some are still under investigation, some trials are continuing, and others are under appeal.

Extraterritorial Legislation as an Arm of International Law

The recognition of territorial sovereignty is a first principle of international law. A state exercises jurisdiction in both criminal and civil matters over persons and property within its territorial limits, and over its ships and aircraft. Offences committed in the state, or on board the ships or aeroplanes of the state, will be tried in the courts of that state. This jurisdiction is called 'territorial jurisdiction'.

When offences are committed *abroad*, the state in which the offender is apprehended may be required to return (extradite) him to the country in which the crime occurred. Some countries will extradite on the basis of a specific treaty, while the legislation of others allows for extradition in response to a request from a foreign government. Such requests are usually granted only where reciprocal arrangements are offered. In general, the principle of double criminality will apply, that is, that the crime for which the offender is being extradited must be also an offence in his own country. Some countries, however, resist the extradition of their own nationals. They prefer to prosecute their citizens at home for offences committed abroad, rather than return them to the country in which they offended. In recent years, even countries that would normally comply with extradition of their nationals have passed legislation permitting them to try offenders under extraterritorial jurisdiction for sexual offences against minors abroad.

There are a number of principles on which extraterritorial legislation may be based:

- the *personality* principle, whereby the state exercises jurisdiction either in the interests of victims who are its nationals (passive personality), or because the wrongdoer is one of its nationals or residents (active personality);
- the *protective* principle, whereby the state seeks to protect its own fundamental interests, whether against its own nationals or non-nationals; and
- the *universality* principle, whereby a state is willing to prosecute certain offences, because these are crimes that the international com-

munity has agreed are universally punishable (for example, piracy, terrorism, torture).

In the cases in this study, only one aspect of territorial jurisdiction applies: the *active personality principle*. Offences were committed against foreign children in other countries, and for whatever reason, the offender has evaded the local jurisdiction. The response is either to prosecute the offender on his home territory, or to have him serve in the country of his nationality or residence the sentence imposed elsewhere.

In order for extraterritorial prosecution to be successful, certain conditions must be fulfilled.

Double criminality This means that the crime committed abroad must be considered an offence in both countries.

Double jeopardy In most countries a person may not be retried for the same offence. (Japan is the exception: a wrongdoer may be tried a second time, but the sentence imposed abroad will be taken into consideration.) This principle applies whether the verdict is a conviction or an acquittal in a foreign tribunal.

Complaint In some countries there are other conditions that must be fulfilled before extraterritorial jurisdiction may apply. Certain countries require a *prior complaint by the victim*, or a request for prosecution by the foreign state.

Which law In most countries, a court applies the law of the country in which the offence is tried. Sweden and Switzerland, however, will apply the sentence of the country in which the offence was committed only if it is more lenient than the relevant national law.

In examining the cases below, and the legislation under which they were prosecuted, three types of modern extraterritorial jurisdiction have been identified.

1. Countries that, *as a general principle*, apply extraterritoriality to offences committed by their citizens abroad. These include Japan, the Netherlands, Norway, Sweden and Switzerland. Extraterritorial jurisdiction can be applied without limitation for certain very serious offences, including those involving the security of the state. With the requirement of double criminality, a large number of other offences, which are more than simple misdemeanours, are also subject to extra-

territoriality. (In Japan double criminality is not a prerequisite for any offences in the Criminal Code that may be prosecuted outside Japan.) In these countries, no special provisions are necessary to deal with child sex tourism, since the legislation already exists.

2. Countries that, *as a general principle*, acknowledge extraterritoriality, but that, in the case of offences against children, have legislated to *facilitate* prosecutions. These countries include Belgium, France and Germany.

3. Countries that have introduced *specific legislation* to cover offences against minors abroad. These include Australia, Ireland and the United Kingdom. The law is restrictive in scope, and applies to clearly defined offences. Double criminality is not required in Australia, but it is in Ireland and the United Kingdom.

The issues define themselves with greater clarity through the cases themselves. These are grouped country by country, according to the nationality of the offender. The names of the offenders have been changed, since it is not the purpose of this work to pursue individuals, or to intensify an already emotionally charged discussion about child abuse in Europe. Indeed, one of the reasons why Europe has taken the lead in prosecuting its nationals who have committed offences against children abroad is perhaps the concern over child abuse, which has, in the 1990s, become symbolic of a deeper and wider malaise in European society.

The Case Histories

1

Tracing the Street-Children

Jan van Schelling: the Netherlands/Philippines

Jan van Schelling, a 43-year-old divorced computer-programmer, visited the Philippines a number of times. During his trips, he arranged for under-age girls to come to his hotel room. He recorded his activities there in pornographic pictures and videos, which he took back to the Netherlands. An investigation into his activities began in February 1996. A local chemist, to whom van Schelling had sent photographs to be developed, reported to the Dutch police that these contained indecent material. In a subsequent police search of his house, further obscene material was found, including 80 videos, photographs and posters of young girls who were naked. Many of these also depicted unlawful sexual acts, committed both in the Netherlands and in the Philippines. This provided the Dutch police with evidence that van Schelling had had unlawful sexual contact with a number of unnamed prostituted children under the age of 12.

In spite of the wealth of photographic and video evidence showing van Schelling with young children, the Dutch police had to find at least one of them. Dutch law allows the police to prosecute an offence under article 245 of the Dutch Criminal Code only if the victim has filed a complaint. Article 245 states that 'any person who performs an indecent act including or constituting the extramarital physical penetration of a minor who has reached the age of twelve but has not yet reached the age of sixteen is liable to a term of imprisonment not exceeding eight years or a fifth category fine'.

In August 1996, the Philippines authorities asked the Dutch to take charge of the case. There was full cooperation between Dutch and Philippines police on the ground in Manila. Dutch police officers went to the Philippines after they had received an official request to do so. No use was made of formal arrangements – the investigation was carried out through direct personal contact and simple cooperation between the Dutch and Philippines police. The police took with them some photographs of the girls and one of the confiscated videos. (They were also investigating a second case of sex tourism, Leo van Engstraat; see case history 2.) In collaboration with the Philippines police, the Australian liaison office in Bangkok and local NGOs, their first task was to trace one or more of the children in the photographs.

Given the number of poor street-children and prostituted children in Manila, locating a child shown in a particular video or photograph is a formidable operation. The police showed the pictures to a worker with a project for street-children in Malate and Quezon City in Metro-Manila. This worker recognized one of the girls as Rita. Interviewed later by the police, Rita confirmed that she had had oral sex with van Schelling. Her statement provided the complaint necessary for a prosecution to proceed in the Netherlands. The girl herself would not have to travel to the Netherlands to give evidence, since this was adequately supplied by the photographs and videos seized by the police. Two specially trained Dutch police officers interviewed her in Manila, in a room where TV and video-link equipment had been installed. Before the hearing, she was accompanied by her mother, who officially made the complaint against the abuser. During the hearing she was alone with the Dutch investigators while her mother waited outside.

Following the identification of Rita, the original statement – that Schelling had infringed article 244 of the Criminal Code by having unlawful sexual contact with a number of Filipina girls under the age of 12 – was amended. Article 244 is substantially the same as article 245, but does not require a formal complaint by the victim. It does, however, require proof that the victim was under 12 years old, and although Rita was under 12 for part of the time-span over which the offences were committed, proof of this might have been more difficult.

On the face of it, article 245 applies only to unlawful sexual contact that takes place in the Netherlands. A separate provision, article 5(1) of the Criminal Code, provides for the extraterritorial application of Dutch law to two categories of offence: first, certain specific crimes such as bigamy, piracy, making oneself unfit for military service, and second, breach of state or business secrets. In these cases, it is not necessary for the country where the acts were committed also to consider them to be offences. Where other types of offence, including those under article 245, are committed outside the Netherlands, Dutch criminal law will apply only if the act is also considered an offence in the territory where it was committed.

The Court found that this double criminality condition was met. Indeed, under Filipino law, penetrative sexual offences are punishable by life imprisonment. The death penalty has recently been restored in the Philippines for heinous crimes, including rape, and rape where the victim is under 18 years old. Acts of lasciviousness against children under 18 are punishable with a term of imprisonment of between 12 and 18 years.

Van Schelling's defence challenged the validity of the statement of the charge against him, and the admissibility of a paragraph subsequently added to the original charge, which acknowledged that the victim was over 12 but under 16 at the time of the offences against her (in fact her twelfth birthday took place during this period). The defence argued that paragraph 6b could not be added to the original paragraph 6, since the offences fell under separate provisions of the Criminal Code (articles 244 and 245) and could not, therefore, have arisen from the same set of facts. The Appeal Court later rejected these arguments.

Van Schelling appeared before the District Court, which is presided over by three judges who give their decision two weeks after the session. There is no jury system in the Netherlands. In October 1996, the District Court in The Hague sentenced Schelling to five years' imprisonment for, among other things, rape and other forms of sexual contacts in the Philippines with a girl under 16. (The maximum would have been eight years' imprisonment.) The sentence also took into account other sexual offences, including rape and sexual contact with women who were unconscious or barely conscious. He had also committed sexual crimes in the Netherlands. The Court did not accept the argument that, because the girl was a prostitute, van Schelling's actions were not criminal. It found that the girl had no free choice, given the economic and social circumstances in which she found herself. There was no evidence of any connection with a broader network of abusers.

Van Schelling appealed on the grounds that the victim had consented to the abuse, and that he had not known her age. The Appeal Court found that the responsibility lay upon him to ascertain the age of the child. In any case, the photographs and videos showed clearly that her body was not fully developed. In a final appeal to the Supreme Court on a point of law, the Appeal Court issued a final judgment in 1998, confirming the sentence. Van Schelling had visited the Philippines on four previous occasions. He is still serving his sentence.

Rita, the victim, was one of six children, four girls and two boys. She was living with her parents, and was said to have been prostituted for about a year. Her father is a construction worker, earning 250 pesos a day (US$8.50). His two sons earn about 150 pesos a day (US$5.10). The house rent was 500 pesos a month, with 200 pesos for electricity and 100 pesos for water. Food costs were about 200 pesos a day. There was no budgetary allowance for any emergency, medical or educational expenses. Rita later took part in the Bahay Tuluyan programmme for street-children. After the case, Wim Kok, the Dutch prime minister, and his wife visited this project, and money was donated to this NGO, which is working with child prostitutes.

A claim for compensation was not made during the criminal procedure, even though this might have been possible under Dutch law. A civil claim was subsequently made in cooperation with Defence for Children International with the help of a Dutch lawyer and the Bahay Tuluyan programme.

The period of limitation in the Netherlands is 12 years. If a child victim submits a complaint, time runs from when he or she is 18. This was the first conviction in the Netherlands for sex crimes committed abroad. It received intense media coverage, and gave rise to a number of TV discussions about sex tourism. Together with the 1996 Stockholm Congress on Child Sex Tourism, this contributed to a greater awareness in the Netherlands of the issues involved.

Attention was also focused on Dutch laws concerning sexual offences against minors. ECPAT Netherlands made suggestions for improvements in the law, consisting of three points: one, that commercial sexual acts with children between the ages of 12 and 16 be punishable without the need for prior complaint; two, that protection be extended to all those under 18; three, that the prior complaint requirement be removed from all cases involving minors below 18: it is not realistic to expect a prostituted child to lay a complaint against a client. The ECPAT proposals refer solely to child prostitution, and are not intended to interfere with the current liberal Dutch law concerning the sexual experiences of young people. In the Netherlands, children over the age of 12 are considered capable of consenting to sexual relations. Nobody will be prosecuted for sexual relations with a child over the age of 12, unless a complaint is made by or on behalf of the child, or the act has involved violence.

ECPAT Netherlands has also launched a campaign against child sex tourism. This has targeted the travel industry, and has involved the distribution of information, brochures and suitcase-labels against the sexual abuse of children. Warnings to travellers about the penalties for such abuse have also been issued. A new draft law was presented to Parliament, which would remove the formal complaint requirement before a prosecution can be brought involving child prostitutes.

2

Buying Girls in Manila

Leo van Engstraat: the Netherlands/Philippines

In December 1995, Leo van Engstraat, a 24-year-old Dutch student, travelled to Manila with a 32-year-old German, Tristram Bleicher (see case history 4). Later, van Engstraat said that the trip had been Bleicher's idea, that he went at Bleicher's invitation, and that Bleicher had paid the travel costs. In Manila both men had sexual encounters with a number of Filipina girls. Through an intermediary they established contact with a nine-year-old girl, Priscilla. This child believed she had been sold to van Engstraat and Bleicher by the grandmother with whom she lived. As a result, Priscilla thought she had no choice in what was done to her, that she 'belonged' to the two men. The offences occurred in the Midland Plaza Hotel in Manila, and the Virra Condominium in Makate, Metro-Manila. A few days later, they travelled together to Cebu, second city of the Philippines, and, once again through an intermediary, they made contact with a 14-year-old, Miranda. Both Priscilla and Miranda were prostituted children. Miranda had already been to Germany for sexual purposes.

The girls travelled with the two Europeans to the Oro Beach resort on the holiday island of Boracay, where they arrived on 8 January 1996. The men rented an apartment. Each had his own room, and each had sexual contact with the girls in turn. They had both oral and vaginal sex with at least one of them, and made videos of some of their acts.

One day, while the girls were sitting outside the apartment, they got into conversation with a woman to whom they confided their situation. This woman, who had been alerted by the hotel owner, was the wife of the mayor of Boracay. Appalled, she contacted the police. On 12 January 1996, local police arrested van Engstraat and Bleicher, charging them with the sexual abuse of minors. Both men later jumped bail (set at

100,000 pesos, or US$3,400), and escaped to Europe by way of Malaysia.

Some three months later, the Filipino authorities asked the Dutch, through the ambassador in Manila, to bring charges against van Engstraat. Representatives of the Dutch police had already been in the Philippines, investigating the case against van Schelling (see case history 1). They had been able to locate both Priscilla and Miranda, and they subsequently arrested van Engstraat. A full delegation, including an investigating magistrate, a public prosecutor and van Engstraat's lawyer, spent a week looking into the case there. There was full cooperation with the Filipino police, who handed over the prosecution file to them. The two girls were interviewed by specially trained Dutch police in Manila, and were by this time under the care of the PREDA Foundation. They were then taken into protective custody by Father Shay Cullen, the Irish priest who runs the PREDA Foundation in Olongapo in the Philippines.[1]

When van Engstraat heard that he was to be prosecuted in the Netherlands, he left the country for southern Europe, but later returned, and, with his lawyer, went to the police in the Netherlands. He gave a statement to the examining judge in anticipation of the outcome of the inquiries in the Philippines.

Although van Engstraat had made videos of some of his activities, he managed to destroy them before the police could seize them. In this way, *prima facie* evidence of the offence was lost. However, the police were able to obtain direct evidence from the two girls. This provided proof that Priscilla was under 12 when the unlawful contact took place, and it furnished the formal complaint required before the police could start proceedings against the abuser of 14-year-old Miranda. The evidence of the girls also supplied details of exactly what had taken place. They did not have to travel to the Netherlands since their presence at the trial was not required.

Van Engstraat was charged before the District Court, under the same circumstances as van Schelling (see case history 1). He was convicted of infringing articles 245 and 247 of the Dutch Criminal Code. Article 245 (as noted in case history 1) prohibits sexual contact, whether physical penetration alone or physical penetration together with other forms of sexual contact, with a child aged between 12 and 16. The formal charges were 1) that, as a Dutch citizen in the Philippines in or around the period from 4 January to 12 January 1996, he had sexual relations (*ontuchtige handelingen*) with a girl named Priscilla; kissed the child's naked body and/or touched her vagina, at least her body; and made her hold his penis and/or let her masturbate him and/or put his penis against her or on her naked vagina (article 244); and 2) that during the same period with a girl called Miranda, then over 12 years of age but under 16, outside marriage, he had sexual contact with her, including sexual intercourse, putting his penis in her vagina or her mouth (article 245).

Article 247 of the Dutch Criminal Code prohibits sexual contact with a child under 16 that does not include physical penetration, and imposes a maximum of six years in prison or a fine. (Sexual contact between married couples when one or both is under 16, is exempt.) As with article 245, article 247 does not ostensibly apply to acts committed outside the Netherlands. As noted in the case of van Schelling, article 5(1) of the Dutch Criminal Code extends the scope of both provisions to cover prohibited acts committed by a Dutch national outside the Netherlands.

Van Engstraat, who had a lawyer and free legal assistance, sought to defend himself on a technicality, namely that there had been no formal transfer of the case by the Philippine authorities to the Dutch, and that this exposed him to a risk of being prosecuted twice. He also questioned whether the prosecution in the Philippines conformed to international standards. He claimed that the discrepancy between the punishments in the Netherlands and the Philippines (far more severe in the latter) invalidated the whole process.

The maximum penalty under article 247 would have been six years' imprisonment, or a maximum fine equivalent to US$50,000; under article 245, eight years' imprisonment or a maximum fine equivalent to US$50,000. The penalty in the Philippines could have been life imprisonment or even death. He was sentenced to two years' imprisonment, of which eight months were suspended, on the condition that he underwent intensive psychiatric treatment.

Van Engstraat appealed against this decision, but it was upheld by the Appeal Court on 17 December 1997. He filed a final appeal before the Dutch Supreme Court on purely formal grounds on 6 January 1998, but this was turned down 11 months later. It was known that van Engstraat had been chairman of a club that openly approved of adults having sex with children. He had been sexually abused in his own youth.

Priscilla was born in Pampanga province in 1986. She is said to have lived formerly in 'the slums of Manila' (*sic*) with her grandmother and sister. Her parents separated and left her and her sister in the care of their elderly grandmother. She is described as 'neglected on account of hardship and abject poverty'. She is said to have been forced into prostitution by a neighbour. She was subsequently placed with the PREDA Residential Centre for Abused Children in Olongapo. Although of school age, she did not attend at the time of the offences. She is now (1999) 14 years old. She recently featured in a TV film, which reported on her progress three years after the offences against her. She is in the same children's home. She said that in the beginning she found life hard, but now she goes to school and is treated well. She used to go onto the streets of Manila whenever she chose, but her movements are more restricted now. She has been in therapy, and has become an activist in the campaign to end sexual abuse of children. She went to Japan to raise awareness of the issue. She says her dream is now to become a police officer or a computer-progammer. She is still afraid of men. She agreed to go with the camera team to the area where she had worked as a prostitute, and became very emotional during the visit.

She told the TV team that when her parents divorced, her aunt and grandmother abused and neglected her. She spent a lot of time on the streets outside the home. When a woman offered her a job cleaning in a hotel, she accepted. The work turned out to be not at all what she had expected, and this is how she entered prostitution. This life lasted for four years. When she recently visited her grandmother and aunt, they showed little interest in her.

Miranda was born in 1981 on the island of Oriental Mindoro, about 250 kilometres from Manila. Her father died when she was 3. At 13, she was sexually abused by her stepfather. She left school in 1994 to work as a travelling salesperson selling cosmetics. When she left this work she stayed in Boracay, where she met some tourists. She was invited by a German national to visit him in Germany, where she was prostituted. She began to work and live on the streets. She is now also at the PREDA Centre.

This was the second case of a Dutch national being prosecuted at home for the abuse of children abroad. The fact that van Engstraat and Bleicher acted in concert makes it all the more extraordinary that there was no cooperation between the Dutch and German authorities over the case. In the case of Bleicher, the victims were compelled to travel to

Germany since their physical presence in the court was necessary. In the Netherlands, hearings in the Philippines and the use of a video-link were sufficient.

Van Engstraat has since served his sentence, and has been released. The whole case lasted from early January 1996 until December 1998, almost three years. There was a considerable amount of media attention, but the victims were well protected.

No claim for compensation was made during the criminal procedure, although this would be possible under Dutch law. A civil claim has been made on behalf of both victims in cooperation with the Defence for Children International.

Note

1. The PREDA (People's Recovery, Empowerment and Development Assistance) Foundation was established by Father Shay Cullen, an Irish Columban missionary, and his colleagues in 1974. It is a member of ECPAT Philippines. It began as a project to save street-children and drug dependants from death squads, who – as has occurred in Brazil and elsewhere – were killing them as a warning to others. PREDA provided sanctuary, therapy, reconciliation and education for street-children. It was not long before PREDA was dealing with sexually abused and prostituted children. Work at the centre involves the teaching of self-respect to the damaged children, together with practical skills in making furniture and other handicraft goods. The centre is at Olongapo, close to the former US military base at Subic Bay, which is still suffering from the legacy of prostitution that arose during the US tenancy of the base – an industry which the government of the Philippines did little to combat. The area swiftly became a destination for sex tourists, a magnet for people from Europe, Australia and the United States who wanted sexual contact with under-age children. Father Cullen campaigned against child abuse by both military personnel and civilian tourists. In the early years it was an uphill struggle against corruption and official indifference. By the time the Americans left Olongapo in 1992, researchers at PREDA estimated that there were 16,000 women and children in prostitution at Olongapo, and the same number in nearby Angeles. Of these, about one in six were minors. Since January 1995, Father Cullen says, there have been 280 successful prosecutions in child sex cases. He has been a consistent campaigner against child sex tourism, and has played a significant role in pressing for the enactment of extraterritorial legislation in Europe and elsewhere.

3

The Community Benefactor

Cees Brijthuis: the Netherlands/Sri Lanka

It was during a police investigation into child abuse committed by Cees Brijthuis in the Netherlands that he was discovered to be in possession of a greal deal of pornographic material depicting South-east Asian children. This included photographs, slides and videos. Brijthuis is described as a divorced 50-year-old swimming instructor and travel agent, and he travelled frequently to South-east Asia. He had visited Sri Lanka a number of times, and had even started a shrimp-processing factory in the country. He was said to be very involved socially in the community at Pothuvil, where he was seen as a benefactor.

In the Netherlands, Brijthuis had had sexual contact with a boy under the age of 16, who had been placed under his supervision as a foster-child for a long period of time. The same pattern had been repeated with a second boy. The case against the offender began when the boy who had been under his supervision returned to his house to be photographed with others by Brijthuis. The boy complained to the police. As a result, when the police searched the house, they found over a hundred videos, photographs and posters of naked young boys, many of them taken in the course of unlawful sexual acts committed in Sri Lanka. On the day of the arrest, a local pharmacy reported that photographs presented by Brijthuis for developing contained obscene material.

Contact between the Dutch and Sri Lankan authorities was established at an official level. Interpol was involved through the Central Intelligence Division of the Dutch police. The Dutch public prosecutor made contact with equivalent officials during the investigation. The public prosecutor, investigating judge and Brijthuis' lawyer later visited Sri Lanka, where they questioned and heard the evidence of the boys. This took place in a local court in Colombo, freeing them from the necessity of having to appear in court in the Netherlands. There was no provision for giving evidence on video. All the members of the Dutch delegation were able to question the boys. Written statements were transmitted to the Netherlands through diplomatic channels.

In spite of Brijthuis' protestations, Dutch police who followed up the case in Sri Lanka found that during his visits there he had also sexually abused boys between the ages of 12 and 16. Five of the victims who appeared on the video-cassettes and photographs were identified by the police. Brijthuis maintained that he did not ask the boys to have sex with him or with each other. He did confess that he had had 'contact' with the boys, but insisted that they often came to see him of their own free will. He was charged under article 247 of the Dutch Criminal Code (see previous case history) with abusing the five Sri Lankan boys, by ordering one or more of the boys to undress in front of him, and to masturbate him or each other, as well as with committing an indecent assault upon them, and forcing them to commit such assaults on each other. He was also charged under article 240b, which covers possession of child pornography. In addition, he was charged with offences against the Dutch boys who had been placed in his care. He admitted these, but continued to deny abuse of the Sri Lankan boys. The police found no evidence that Brijthuis formed part of a wider network. He appeared to have made the trips and to have assembled the pornographic material for his own satisfaction and pleasure.

Brijthuis was charged before the District Court, where three judges make a decision two weeks after the session. He confessed to the sexual abuse of the Dutch boys in his care, but continued to deny that he had incited the Sri Lankan boys to have sex with each other or with him. He said the boys had come to him of their own volition. Diaries were exhibited, kept by Brijthuis and detailing where he was each day and with whom he met. It is assumed that he paid his own lawyer.

The boys against whom the offences were committed came from a small village. It is stated that 'they have been damaged by the sexual abuse, which is frowned upon in their community, and will have difficulties in finding work and a wife in later years'. Whatever the truth of this observation, what is not at issue is the nature of the offences, and the influence that a wealthy Westerner exercised over poor children when he induced them to make pornographic videos. He not only abused the boys sexually himself, but encouraged or compelled them to perform sexual acts with each other, and filmed these activities. He gave the boys presents, food and small amounts of money.

The five children had all been positively identified from the video material. They were all between the ages of 11 and 14 at the time of the offences. All lived in the same village of Pothuvil. Their occupations/education are described as 'unknown'. The social circumstances are laconically reported as 'poor families'. Whether they received any 'treatment' or other guidance following the abuse is not known.

On 13 November 1997, the Utrecht District Court sentenced Brijthuis to five years' imprisonment for, *inter alia*, having sexual contact with boys under 16, including five in Sri Lanka. The public prosecutor had sought a sentence of six years, which would have been the maximum under article 247 (or a fine of the equivalent of US$25,000). Under article 240b, three months' imprisonment would have been the maximum for the production or possession of child pornography.

In Sri Lanka, the offence is also a crime (article 365a of the Penal Code) and the penalty there would have been higher. At the end of October 1995, vice laws in Sri Lanka became more stringent. Under a new article 258a, it is a criminal offence to permit children under 18 to pose obscenely. This means that it would be possible now for the Dutch public prosecutor to handle a case of the creation or making of child pornographic material.

Brijthuis made a submission to the Appeal Court in Amsterdam, which upheld the decision of the District Court. He then filed a further appeal to the Supreme Court on 1 September 1998.

For the first time, a request made on behalf of the five boys for compensation was successful, and the Court ordered Brijthuis to pay the equivalent of US$750 to each victim. The victims were represented by an official of the Court. This was the maximum that could be awarded to a victim in a criminal case under the law as it was at the time when the offences were committed. This limit was lifted under legislation that came into force in April 1995. The period of limitation is 12 years, which, if the victim has made a complaint, runs from when he or she reaches the age of 18.

Brijthuis is at present in prison. He is – as he mentioned in his appeal to the High Court of Appeal in Amsterdam – socially and financially ruined. This was the fourth conviction in the Netherlands for sexual offences against children outside the national territory. Media attention was considerable in the wake of the Stockholm Congress, and a national plan of action to combat the commercial sexual exploitation of children was awaited late in 1999 or early 2000.

There was further legal fallout from this case. A decision by the High Court of Appeal in April 1996 declared that possession of child pornography (even if not for distribution) was also a criminal offence. The case began in early 1996 and the sentence was handed down in November 1997. It was confirmed by the Supreme Court in July 1998, and a further appeal was withdrawn.

4

On the Holiday Island

Tristram Bleicher: Germany/Philippines

In December 1995, Tristram Bleicher, a 32-year-old, self-employed owner of an electronics business, went to the Philippines as a tourist. He was accompanied by a Dutch acquaintance (Leo van Engstraat; see case history 2). On the evening of 4 January 1996, Bleicher arranged for a girl (whom he assumed to be 9 years old; she was actually aged 11) to be brought to him in his room in the Midland Plaza Hotel in Manila. The girl was brought by a female intermediary. He agreed a fee with this woman, set up a video camera on a stand, and connected a small monitor to it. He then fully undressed the girl, touched her and forced her to masturbate him. He recorded the whole process. A few days later, he arranged for the girl to be brought to him again. He made an agreement with the woman intermediary to keep the girl with him for several days, so that he could fly with her to the holiday island of Boracay, 400 kilometres from Manila.

The child was unable to communicate verbally with Bleicher in any way. With the help of the go-between, a second girl was engaged to go with them as translator. Before leaving Manila, Bleicher took both girls to his room in an apartment complex. He asked his companion to bring the video equipment into the room. Bleicher set up the video, undressed the girl and undressed himself. He again touched her indecently. He tied the girl to the bedpost. He filmed all this. The girl carried out Bleicher's instructions hesitantly and unwillingly. She was very frightened, but did as she was told, because she feared worse would happen when she was tied up. The second girl told her that Bleicher had paid for her, and could do with her whatever he chose.

Bleicher and his companion, Leo van Engstraat, travelled to Boracay with the two girls in January 1996. The took two rooms in a hotel close to the beach. Bleicher shared his room with the girl. On 10 January, the accused and his companion were observed by the hotel owner: they were conspicuous because of the under-age girls staying in their rooms. The hotel owner expressed his concern to the wife of the mayor, who alerted the local police. The police called in the National Bureau of Investigation, which had been established in Manila for the purpose of combating child prostitution. An investigating agent flew to Boracay and interviewed the two children and other witnesses.

Criminal charges were then brought by the victims against the accused on 12 January 1996, under the responsibility of the Public Prosecutor's Office in Kalibo, Alkan province. The charge was violation of the Republic Act 7610, which is a law for the protection of children against abuse, discrimination and exploitation. Bleicher was accused of violation of article 336 in relation to RA 7610. The two children were supported by an agent from the National Bureau of Investigation.

The two girls were witnesses. Further evidence was provided by a female social worker from the Philippines Social Ministry, by Father Shay Cullen, in whose centre the girls have found refuge (see note 1, case history 2), by the police agent from the special unit against child prostitution, and by a female court psychologist who vouched for the credibility of the victims as witnesses. During the course of the court proceedings in the Philippines, the Netherlands and Germany, the 11-year-old had to give evidence on several occasions: to the police, to the Public Prosecutor's Office, to the Court in Manila (in the case of van Engstraat, for which Dutch officials travelled to the Philippines), and to the German Court.

Having been charged, the two men were granted bail on 25 January 1996 (a sum of US$1,700 each). They then fled the Philippines via Malaysia. It may seem extraordinary that, given the bureaucratic apparatus deployed by the authorities to charge the accused, they were so readily granted bail, and so easily left the country. This also raises an issue that is encountered several times in the cases, and that is the possibilities that exist for the privileged to evade jurisdiction in the countries where the offences are committed. The opportunities for bribery, personal contact with the elite by those of high social standing, the reluctance of certain authorities to pursue influential foreigners – these amount to a powerful argument for the tightening of extraterritorial legislation in Europe and elsewhere.

Following newspaper publicity in the Philippines, the case came to the attention of the authorities in Germany, thanks to the intervention of a German TV crew. Investigations began on 2 February 1996, when, following a request for evidence from the German public prosecutor, the Philippine charges were conveyed by the German federal minister of justice to the minister of justice of the state of North Rhine-Westphalia. Bleicher was remanded in custody on 23 August 1996.

A number of NGOs assisted the prosecution by providing the public prosecutor with background information. These included ECPAT Germany (Arbeitsgemeinschaft gegen kommerzielle sexuelle Ausbeutung von Kindern), Terre des Hommes and PREDA in the Philippines.

Bleicher was brought to trial in the District Court (*Amtsgerischt*), the lowest court, with one professional magistrate and two lay assessors. He was found to have been in violation three times of article 176 of the Criminal Code, sexual abuse of a minor under the age of 14. Child abuse may be punished in Germany whether or not it is an offence in the country in which it is committed. The same is true of the distribution of child pornography. In other cases, German criminal law is applicable only when the offence committed is a criminal offence in Germany as well as in the country where it is committed. The punishment in Germany for child abuse may be from six months to ten years. The court procedure in the Philippines was suspended, since the accused had fled the country. The penalty in the Philippines would probably have been far more severe (see case history 2). Changes have subsequently been made to German criminal law. Among other things, the maximum penalty for a number of sex crimes has been increased, and a new victim protection law has been in operation since April 1998. Any imprisonment based on a foreign verdict and imposed abroad is taken into account in a criminal trial in Germany, and will be deducted from any further sentence. Any other period of incarceration abroad – for example, during the investigation – will also be deducted from time served in Germany.

In Germany, Bleicher offered no defence. He refused to answer the charges, and kept silent throughout the proceedings. He was sentenced to three years and six months in prison. An appeal was lodged with a superior court (*Landgericht*), but on intervention by the public prosecutor's office and the lawyer for the co-accuser (the victim), the appeal was withdrawn, and the sentence confirmed. Bleicher has served his sentence. Nothing is known of his life afterwards. He was not given any supervision on his release.

This was the first conviction in Germany for sex crimes committed outside the country. It was also the first time a witness had been brought to Germany to give evidence in court. She had already given evidence to the police in Manila, to the Public Prosecutor's Office and to the Court in Manila in the case of Leo van Engstraat. She travelled to Germany to be present at the trial in the company of a female carer, and was required to make a statement as witness on only one day in the five-day trial. She was represented by a woman lawyer, who successfully applied to the Court to prevent her from having to face the accused. Members of the public were allowed to attend the trial, but were excluded when the child witnesses were examined. Filming, photography and sound recording were not allowed.

There was considerable press criticism of the fact that the child had been brought to Germany, with all the bewildering and unfamiliar experiences involved in such a journey. Although she was well looked after, and Father Shay Cullen insisted that she, too, wanted justice, it remains questionable whether such an ordeal relieves or compounds the distress the child has already endured.

The girl was 11 at the time of the offence. She was born in 1984, 'probably' in Manila. Although she had received some primary education, she was not attending school at the time of the offence. The whereabouts of her mother were unknown. She is described as being 'of a poor family', and to have earned money 'by selling perfume to tourists'. After the trial, she returned to the PREDA home, run by Father Shay Cullen, where she still lives (see case history 2). It is reported that 'she has followed therapy and goes to school' (the researcher adds 'as far as is known'). No decision was made on compensation, which is being claimed separately by the victim under civil law (the equivalent of US$3,300).

The period of limitation is related to the maximum sentence with which the crime is punishable. The limitation starts from the moment the most recent of the crimes was committed; in this case, the period of limitation is three years. The time from the offence, in January 1996, to the date of sentencing, in December 1996, was less than a year. This did not prevent questions from being asked in the German Parliament concerning delays in the case. In fact, this was one of the shortest periods from the offence to sentencing of any of the cases; any slight delay was caused by the need to obtain evidence from the Philippines.

5

A Conflict of Interests

Vinzenz Berger: Switzerland/Sri Lanka

On 25 June 1998, Vinzenz Berger, a 55-year-old businessman, was convicted by the Zurich District Court of having had unlawful sexual contact over a period of some years with a number of boys born between 1976 and 1985 in Sri Lanka. Until the 1970s, Berger had a radio and television business in Zurich. He had visited Sri Lanka on holiday a number of times, and when a group of Sri Lankan investors were lobbying for Swiss investment in their country he did not hesitate. He wound up his company in Zurich, and transferred his business interests to Sri Lanka, setting up various electronics companies. He opened an electronic switch factory close to Negombo, which provided about 1,500 jobs, and he also established a shrimp-processing plant.

Berger also owned a substantial property in Etukula, close to Negombo, about 50 kilometres north of Colombo, and had constructed other properties. He was seen as a man of substance, highly respected in Sri Lanka. He maintained good social relations with members of the elite, the bureaucracy, police and political parties. He was perceived as a social benefactor because of his sponsorship and financial support of schools and churches. He even gave help to official institutions, such as the local police offices, and he established a health centre for children in his own house and a school for young people.

Berger abused boys systematically over some time, an abuse that followed a distinctive pattern. He invited boys between the ages of 11 and 15 or allowed his servants or guests to invite them to his villa, and permitted them to play in the garden and swim in the pool. He also offered them food. When the boys became familiar with the surroundings, he encouraged them to come inside the house to the television room and the bedroom. There he persuaded them to watch pornographic films, in which sex between adults and children appeared normal. The boys were also compelled to submit to a variety of sexual acts. While watching the films, Berger would undress them, touch their penises or masturbate them. He had oral sex with the boys or had them perform oral sex on him. With three of the boys, Berger established long-term relationships that lasted for several years. He did not belong to any organized network.

As a reward for their sexual services, the boys were given presents, money for school, schoolbooks, clothes and shoes. He sometimes gave them money to spend on themselves. Berger's abusive behaviour with children continued over a considerable period. He claimed that his relationship with the boys was known, considered normal and accepted, until the local people turned against him. By the end of the 1980s, his behaviour was being questioned because he was always surrounded by boys. In 1989 he was visited by a member of the local council and an MP, who made it clear to him that his conduct would no longer be tolerated. Nothing further came of this, at least at the official level. Quite the contrary: when some parents and church leaders sought an official investigation, they were threatened by Berger.

But popular suspicions were not so easily allayed. In 1992–93, several campaigns were waged against Berger. These, in turn, provoked counter-campaigns in his support – some of them involving parents of the children he had abused. A rumour spread that HIV was being disseminated through his health centre, and this forced him to close it down. In 1996, notices were posted telling Berger to 'leave our children alone' and 'go home.' The Sri Lankan authorities took no action against him, because he was too influential, and too many people depended on him for employment. In view of the negative publicity generated throughout the world by this case, President Chandrika Kumaratunga assumed responsibility, setting up a task force to press local authorities in Sri Lanka to deal with the issue of the sexual exploitation of children.

It took the intervention of Sri Lankan and Swiss NGOs before a police investigation was begun, a process that led to the arrest of Berger in Sri Lanka. In 1992, PEACE (Protecting Environment and Children Everywhere, the Sri Lankan representative of ECPAT International) had inaugurated a study on child prostitution in Sri Lanka. The remit of this was to look at commercial sexual exploitation of children, and to investigate the activities of certain foreigners in the communities where they were living. The case of Berger came within the scope of this study, although his name was not mentioned in the report.

PEACE sent the findings, with additional material, to Switzerland, to ECPAT. The latter, which did not have the funds to pursue it further, passed the dossier to CIDE (Comité international pour la dignité de l'enfant). In 1996, two journalists from CIDE travelled to Sri Lanka specifically to conduct further research into the activities of the wealthy Swiss expatriate. They interviewed several boys. Their report was passed on to the Swiss Federal Police, the section concerned with trafficking in human beings. Personal contact was made with the authorities in Sri Lanka by a high-ranking police officer. After investigations in Switzerland, a copy of the report was sent through Interpol to the authorities in Sri Lanka, and Berger was arrested in October 1996.

Berger was under arrest for two weeks, and quickly released on bail. The media in Sri Lanka publicized the case and its importance, depending, as it did, on the fact that the Zurich prosecutor had passed information on Berger to the Sri Lankan authorities. News of this was transmitted to the Zurich prosecutor, who drew up questions for PEACE so that a criminal case could be opened in Switzerland. Among the questions PEACE asked was why Berger had been released, on what legal basis, and how much he had paid in surety for bail. No answer was received, and PEACE did not have the resources to find out.

A further court hearing was set. Berger mustered all the support he could, in order to get prominent politicians and police officers to support him in having the charges dismissed. The hearing was again postponed until February 1997. ECPAT Switzerland and CIDE drew up a letter to the Zurich prosecutor, setting out in detail the events as they had unfolded in Sri Lanka. The Swiss authorities were inhibited from proceeding, since the case was pending in Sri Lanka. In February 1997, Sri Lanka unexpectedly declared Berger *persona non grata* and deported him to Switzerland. Although the Swiss would have preferred him to be tried and convicted in Sri Lanka where the offences were committed, they nevertheless arrested him on his arrival. The Sri Lankan authorities kept the Swiss informed about the deportation, including Berger's flight number. The Swiss authorities then requested legal assistance from Sri Lanka, so that evidence there could be located by Swiss investigating teams. The Sri Lankans established contact with the victims and made them available for interview.

The Zurich investigators went to Sri Lanka to question victims and witnesses. The Swiss investigating authorities conducted their inquiries with considerable sensitivity towards the children. The victims did not have to face the offender in court, and their testimonies were recorded on video. They were interviewed by the Swiss prosecutor, who later said that his team had had to operate in conditions that were barely tolerable, since they had to travel daily from Colombo, they had to wait for faxes to be sent, and there was much delay and waiting around. The hearings were held in a hotel room in Negombo, and certainly did not accord with the conditions that would have been demanded by Switzerland. There were sometimes as many as ten adults present during the hearings. The questioning of the boys took three to four hours. However, the questions were clear and direct, and the boys were allowed breaks for refreshments. Some of the boys appeared to have been tutored by supporters of Berger, and were uninformative. The others, once they had overcome their apprehension, were more open in their replies. Berger was in preventive detention in Switzerland, and received daily reports of the hearings by fax. This enabled him to ask additional questions. His legal representative was present in Negombo during the hearings of the boys.

Berger was formally charged in February 1998 under Section 187 of the Swiss Criminal Code, which deals with sexual acts with children. Article 6 is the relevant statute dealing with extraterritorial offences. It appears that he cooperated with the inquiries, and his case came to trial quickly, in June of the same year. He was convicted by the District Court of Zurich, a chamber of three judges. The evidence consisted of reports and interviews by the police and NGOs, as well as the interviews conducted by the Swiss investigating officers with the children in Sri Lanka. In accordance with Swiss law, there was no confrontation between the offender and his victims, who were not required to appear in court in Switzerland.

Berger had committed the offences between 1984 and 1996. In 1995, the Sri Lankan Penal Code was amended. Before the amendment, the maximum penalty for the abuse of children would have been two years; this was increased in 1995 to 20 years. In Switzerland, the principle of applying the more lenient law in favour of the offender applies in extraterritorial offences (*lex mitior*, article 6 of the Swiss Penal Code). The Sri Lankan law was applied for offences up to 1995, and the Swiss law for those after 1995.

As a result of the case, the period of limitation for sexual offences against children has been increased in Sri Lanka from five to ten years. In Switzerland, changes in the law under preparation include the criminalization of the possession of pornography depicting the sexual exploitation of children; the liability of travel agencies; the extension of extraterritorial legislation to cover all habitual residents of Switzerland as well as its nationals; and the abolition of double criminality as a precondition for extraterritorial legislation.

Berger's defence was that he cooperated with the investigation. He insisted that the customs of Sri Lanka differed from those in Switzerland, and that his behaviour was regarded as normal, since boys would openly proposition foreigners because of their poverty. He denied that he had acted with intent to corrupt. He claimed that Sri Lanka had done nothing to prevent sex tourism, and believed he had been arrested only because of the pressure exercised by the BBC, who had made a TV film about him. The defence also questioned the role of the NGOs in the investigation: there was a risk of partiality in their cooperation with the media. The defence requested that the disturbed background of the offender should be taken into consideration.

He was sentenced to four and a half years' imprisonment (with hard labour), and was required to undergo psychiatric treatment (he had done this on a voluntary basis before the trial). The limitation period on some of his acts had expired. The victims were represented by a female Swiss lawyer, who claimed full compensation in accordance with Swiss law on aid to victims. Whether or not this compensation law applies to foreign victims did not, however, come to the test in this case, since Berger offered to pay damages himself (however, at the time of writing he has not yet paid). He was ordered to pay the boys concerned a total of CHF 61,000 (about US$39,000). Berger also offered to pay CHF 50,000 (about US$32,000) to child protection organizations in Sri Lanka. In court, he apologized to the children. This was the first time a Swiss national had been convicted in Switzerland for sexual abuse of children committed exclusively abroad.

Berger had an unhappy childhood. For decades he had had no contact with his father, but was brought up by his grandparents and in children's homes. While in these homes, he had been sexually abused regularly by older boys. He had been convicted in Switzerland many years previously for paedophile offences, but had received only a mild sentence.

Fifteen boys whose names were known were involved, all born between 1976 and 1985. Their place of birth is reported without detail as 'Sri Lanka'. Most are described as having had 'a few years' primary education'. The parents were 'mostly' the legal guardians. Almost all the boys came from the lowest social stratum. 'They often said' that their fathers were fishermen and their mothers housewives. The families had very low incomes and were in frequent financial trouble. In some cases the parents knew what was happening to their boys and they received money for it.

The Berger episode became a test case in Switzerland, and it was regarded as important both domestically and abroad. It demonstrated that extraterritorial legislation is effective, and it signalled to Sri Lanka – and other countries – that the status of the offender should not inhibit the full rigour of proceedings against him.

The story received a great deal of media attention, both in Switzerland and Sri Lanka. A BBC documentary about the case was shown on Swiss television before the trial.

Berger is at present serving his sentence, and taking advantage of the therapy that is available. He is banned for life from entering Sri Lanka, and his assets there are still being liquidated. The time-frame covered by the whole case, from its inception to the judgment in June 1998, is about ten years.

6

Tangled Responsibilities

Alexander Langenscheidt: Germany and Switzerland/ the Philippines and the Czech Republic

Alexander Langenscheidt is a German engineer, born in Leipzig in 1934. A highly respected man, an honorary professor in Dresden, he also owned an international micro-electronics company. At his former homes, in Zurich and Turin, he was described by neighbours as a polite, helpful and ordinary man.

In November 1995, Langenscheidt was arrested in the Philippines. The police in Pasay City received a tip-off from a concerned citizen, who had observed a pimp make a deal with a foreigner to whom he promised to supply a young girl. The police visited the place where this transaction occurred and arrested four young men on suspicion of pimping. One of these informed the police that a certain 'Minda' was offering her daughter to foreigners. The police traced Minda, and found her just as she was getting into a taxi in which Langenscheidt and the girl, a 12-year-old, were sitting. All three were taken to the police station and interviewed. The girl then underwent a gynaecological examination, and was sent to an institution. Langenscheidt and the mother were remanded in custody. Langenscheidt was charged by the Filipino authorities with repeated unlawful sexual contact with the girl. He was also charged with the production and distribution of pornographic videos.

He was released on bail of 200,000 pesos (US$6,400). With the help of the German Embassy, he was issued with a new passport. He escaped from the Philippines to Germany, and later, to Switzerland. Questions about this were asked in the German Parliament. Details were demanded of the procedure followed by German Embassies in cases of offences alleged against Germans abroad. The then government, in its reply, stated that according to law, Embassies are obliged to provide German nationals with a passport or a substitute passport, although limits on this are possible if the prevention of criminal acts is at issue.

Less than a year later, Langenscheidt was arrested on one of his visits to the Czech Republic. He visited the country on many occasions betwen 1994 and 1996. Dresden is only about one hour's drive from the Bohemia region of the Czech Republic. The Czech authorities charged him with unlawful sexual contact with at least nine girls between the ages of 5 and 17, and with on a number of occasions deflowering the girls involved. He was also charged with the production and distribution of pornographic videos, as well as having drugged the girls into submission. Most of the victims were Roma children, that is the children of Gypsies, the poorest and most discriminated against group in the Czech Republic. Most of the offences were committed in Litomerice. Significantly, the arrest of Langenscheidt in the Czech Republic followed a complaint to the police by a girl who was brought to Langenscheidt, but who was also rejected by him. The girl turned to a member of her family, an 'uncle'. This man considered that Langenscheidt should be made to pay, even though no sexual contact had occurred. He went to the hotel where Langenscheidt was staying, but was unceremoniously turned away by him. The uncle alerted the police, and together with the rejected girl, laid charges against Langenscheidt for rape and deprivation of liberty. When the police went to the hotel, they found him in his room, involved in unlawful sexual contact with three girls between the ages of 12 and 15. He was recording his activities on video. Langenscheidt was arrested on the spot. This was August 1996.

The Czech authorities formally asked the Swiss for assistance in the case. The Swiss authorities provided them with incriminating videotapes, which they had seized from Langenscheidt's apartment in Zurich. The Swiss police were aware of his earlier arrest in the Philippines, and the search produced about eight hundred videos. Approximately one hundred of these contained evidence of unlawful sexual activity, some with Filipino children. The Swiss authorities then began an investigation into the activities of Langenscheidt. They subsequently found films and magazines dating from the 1980s, some of which Langenscheidt had kept in a bank safe. When NGOs brought to the attention of the Zurich investigating authorities the international dimension of the case, they began to cooperate with their colleagues in the Philippines and the Czech Republic. For instance, they made information informally available to the Filipino authorities, which could have been used as a basis for a formal request for legal assistance from Switzerland. In February 1997, the consulate of the Philippines in Switzerland asked for permission to examine the videos. Switzerland then informed authorities in the Philippines of the formalities required for legal assistance. The Consulate-General was provided with everything necessary for the Filipino authorities to expedite a letter of request for assistance. Hearing nothing, the Swiss Federal Police Department again explained the procedure for legal assistance. Hearings in the Philippines into the case have been repeatedly postponed. Cooperation between the four countries involved has proved very variable, often cumbersome and bureaucratic.

Between the Czech Republic and Switzerland information was first exchanged through police channels. A letter of request was passed to Switzerland by the Czech authorities in March 1997, requesting that the videos be handed over to the Czech Republic. Interpol had originally reported Langenscheidt's arrest in the Czech Republic to Germany, which, in turn, reported it to Switzerland. In Germany, the charges in the Philippines were known, and an arrest warrant against Langenscheidt was issued immediately. In November 1996, Switzerland asked that the Czech Republic be allowed to interview Langenscheidt. This interview was conducted in April 1997 by the Czech public prosecutor in the presence of the Zurich district prosecutor.

In October 1996, Germany sent a letter to Switzerland requesting access to the videos. In November 1997, following correspondence about the status of the investigation, rolls of film, videos and other documents were sent to the German authorities.

In January 1998, Langenscheidt appeared in a court in the Czech Republic. The statute under which he was charged is not known, but he was accused of administering heroin, abducting of minors and committing sexual acts with minors. He was sentenced to two and a half years' hard labour. The fact that this was a case of prostitution served as a mitigating factor, even though young children were involved. Both Langenscheidt and the public prosecutor have appealed: the offender against conviction, and the public prosecutor against his acquittal on charges of drug abuse. There was cooperation between the Swiss and Czech authorities, although it required some pressure from the Swiss upon their Czech counterparts. Langenscheidt presumably remains in custody in the Czech Republic. If Germany had not issued a warrant for his arrest, he could have been released on bail. The warrant expired in July 1998. A request was made for an extension by the Czech public prosecutor, who is demanding a five-year jail sentence.

In his defence in this trial, Langenscheidt claimed he had a special interest in Romany culture, and that he had offered financial support to the girls' families. He retains two lawyers in the Czech Republic, one in Switzerland and one in Germany. The German authorities have so far released no information on the progress of their investigation. The role of the German Embassy is significant since it was instrumental in Langenscheidt's escape from the Philippines, which provided him with an opportunity for further unlawful activities. Langenscheidt is also under investigation in Switzerland; whether he has committed any offences there is not yet known. The Swiss authorities were crucial in the case: after consulting NGOs, they made an effort to coordinate international cooperation by offering support to all the countries involved. Most of the evidence against Langenscheidt is held in Switzerland, in the form of video-tapes.

National authorities found that both their own national legislation and administrative practices acted as a hindrance to the bringing of effective proceedings against Langenscheidt. This led to a delay even in deciding which authority was responsible for various aspects of the case. Each country was in possession of only a fragment of the whole story: thus, the Czech authorities based their proceedings only on the evidence they had collected, in spite of the fact that further evidence on tape was available. In any case, a clash of political, legal and cultural perceptions (for example, the fact that prostitution of children is a mitigating factor in the Czech Republic) offers wrongdoers a number of loopholes through which they can escape.

Cooperation between Germany and Switzerland was the easiest, since they have a bilateral agreement on legal assistance that can by-pass formal diplomatic channels. Between Switzerland and the Czech Republic there are relatively good provisions, since Swiss officers may travel to the Czech Republic to question suspects. Switzerland has sought informal cooperation with the Philippines, but, as explained above, the authorities there have so far not sought legal assistance from Switzerland.

In any case, formal methods of seeking such assistance are cumbersome. Bilateral conventions speed up the process. More imaginative and proactive steps should be taken to improve communication between countries in these matters. Two NGOs in Switzerland and one in the Philippines exerted pressure to accelerate action by the authorities.

There are further questions. Article 6 of the Swiss Criminal Code applies only to Swiss citizens, not to foreigners domiciled in Switzerland. It is also unclear whether German extraterritorial legislation applies to Langenscheidt, since although he is a German citizen, he has not lived there for many years. In Germany, the witnesses have to appear in court (as in the case of Bleicher). Since the Czech victims were without fixed abode, it would prove difficult to bring them to Germany to testify.

Another legal problem arose in Switzerland. At the time, it was not an offence to possess child pornography, and it is unclear whether the Swiss could charge Langenscheidt for producing, importing and (possibly) dealing in child pornography. Proposals to amend the law are proceeding.

The offender is described as an engineer, an honorary professor of micro-electronics in Dresden, and owner of an internationally known micro-electronics company. He is said to have been 'familiar in the highest circles in Germany'. It is further stated that although it must have been known at the highest level in the judiciary that Langenscheidt was involved in the sexual exploitation of children in the Philippines, the German authorities neglected to take steps against him when he fled from the Philippines to Germany, and then travelled on to Zurich in Switzerland. In Zurich, Langenscheidt was known as a 'polite, courteous and unobtrusive person'. There were suspicions that there had been a case against him in Ireland in the early 1980s, but the outcome of that case is unknown.

The first victim, in the Philippines, was 12 years old at the time the offences against her were committed. She had had one year of schooling. Parental authority was exercised by the mother, but she was also without a fixed address. The father has either left the family or is dead. The mother had 'apparently' remarried. The girl is described as 'a streetchild'. She was introduced to Langenscheidt by a 'friend', and it was the mother herself who finally brought her to him. The mother denied that she was aware that Langenscheidt was sexually exploiting her daughter. As far as she knew, he was only filming and photographing the girl. He gave the girl 1,000–2,000 pesos each time (US$32–64). She gave this money to her mother, who used it to buy clothing and daily necessities.

The perfunctory details about most of the children and their lives is one of the most serious flaws in the ways many of the cases in the book were pursued. There is a serious moral issue here, which cuts across the concern with the ramifications involved in setting up legal mechanisms to facilitate pursuit of the abusers. If people without resources or shelter live on city streeets, surely a primary concern should be the rehabilitation of those so vulnerable that they will even collude with crimes committed against their children. The fact that the girl in this case was sent to 'an institution' should scarcely reassure us. In any case, it may well be asked how you rehabilitate those who were never 'habilitated' in the first place – whatever that may mean.

As far as the Roma children in the Czech Republic are concerned, it is stated that some were pupils in a 'special' school; the educational status of the rest is unknown. One of the girls lived with her grand-mother. Others apparently lived in homes, and yet others with their clans. It is stated that Langenscheidt was mainly interested in Romany girls, some of whom he fetched from homes. Others were brought to him by clan members. Langenscheidt 'supported' the families and the homes, yet he is said to have been mean, and bargained for lower prices for the girls. He was also accused of giving them heroin. According to the services they rendered, they were paid from 4,000 to 50,000 Czech Crowns (US$115–1,380), the latter sum having been offered for virgins, for whom he had an apparent preference.

This case illustrates clearly the contrast between the ease with which privileged travellers can move around the world, and the obstacles to administrative efficiency between countries jealous of their national sovereignties, and without mechanisms for speedy cooperation with others in the pursuit of offenders. For tactical reasons, it has been decided to concentrate on the gravest crimes, which were those com-mitted in the Czech Republic, in spite of the fact that the prostitution of children there is held to be a mitigating circumstance.

The authorities in Zurich did seize some of Langenscheidt's assets. But since neither the Philippines nor the Czech Republic demanded extradition of the offender, the money had to be returned to Langen-scheidt. The authorities held back some of this money to cover the costs to themselves of pursuing the case. Langenscheidt has appealed against the retention of these funds. That case is still pending.

Langenscheidt was subsequently tried *in absentia* in the Philippines, and sentenced to indefinite detention. This occurred only late in 1999, while he was still in jail in the Czech Republic. His release was due in January 2000. The effect of the case upon possible conviction in the Philippines is not yet clear. There seemed to be a number of possibilities: a formal request by the Philippines for him to be sent there to serve his sentence, or a request from the authorities in the Philippines to the Czech Republic or to Germany for him to serve his sentence in these countries. The magistrate responsible for the case in Switzerland indicated to a worker from ECPAT Switzerland (the Swiss NGO set up to fight the commercial exploitation of children) that proceedings against him had been dropped. The reason for this was the fact that the offence committed in Switzerland (possession of child pornography) is still not a crime in Switzerland, and since he has already spent three years in jail in the Czech Republic, any possible sentence handed down in Switzerland would be covered by this period of incarceration.

The NGO in the Philippines that was in liaison with ECPAT Switzerland in Switzerland subsequently reported that a liaison officer from the German Embassy in Bangkok visited the Philippines and took two of Langenscheidt's video-tapes from the Filipino prosecutor, stating that these would be used to facilitate a prosecution in Germany. No receipt was given, and indeed, the statement was untrue. The victim's lawyer was unable to get the tapes back through the Department of Foreign Affairs. The NGO sent a strongly worded letter to Bangkok. Two blank tapes were then returned through the Department of Foreign Affairs.

7

The Violence of the 'Child-Lovers'

Andreas Pfister and Theophilus Konrad Waldvogel: Switzerland/Sri Lanka

In February 1995, the police found two Swiss citizens, Andreas Pfister and Theophilus Konrad Waldvogel, committing unlawful sexual acts with two 12-year-old boys, Naranjan and Mullu, in an apartment at Piliyandala, a beach resort near Colombo in Sri Lanka. All four were naked. Police had responded to a tip-off, and the senior superintendent of police headquarters in Colombo ordered the raid on the apartment. The Swiss Department of Foreign Affairs was immediately informed of the arrests through the Swiss Embassy in Colombo, although what the Embassy knew was obtained from the press. As more details emerged, these were passed on to the Swiss Department of Justice.

About a week after their arrest, the two men were released on bail. The level of surety was the equivalent of US$33 – an absurdly low sum. After their release, Pfister remained in Sri Lanka, while Waldvogel escaped to Switzerland. It is not known how Waldvogel got out of Sri Lanka – his passport had been confiscated by the authorities. Interpol informed the Sri Lankan authorities once Waldvogel had returned to Switzerland.

Although the Sri Lankan authorities laid charges against Pfister and Waldvogel for unlawful sexual contact with the boys, the proceedings were extremely protracted, and the hearings were postponed about fifteen times in the following two years. Such delays are not uncommon in Sri Lanka – trials usually take place only if all offenders, prosecutors and witnesses are present; otherwise, the trial is suspended. Although no official information was available, it is believed that the two men were charged with 'immoral behaviour' and 'spreading sexual diseases'. In 1997, both offenders were convicted and sentenced to two years' imprisonment, the maximum penalty according to the law at the time when the offences were committed. In Switzerland, offenders are liable to a maximum punishment of five years' imprisonment for sexual acts with children.

Pfister was present at the hearing, but Waldvogel was convicted *in absentia*. This is possible under Sri Lankan law when the evidence is sufficiently strong, and in any case, his accomplice was present. Pfister pleaded not guilty. He said he loved children, and was helping them and their parents. He twice contacted a Sri Lankan NGO, explaining that he supported their work and did not see himself as an offender.

Before the hearings in Sri Lanka, the Swiss authorities had investigated Waldvogel. He became a suspect in Switzerland, as a consequence of a telephone tapping against another individual who was believed to be involved in pornography. Charges had been brought against him in 1994, but these were dismissed for lack of evidence. As a result, however, Waldvogel lost his job as a teacher. Further charges were brought in 1996, but again there was a lack of evidence. It was recognized that Waldvogel was an offender, but the Swiss authorities have never had sufficient evidence to lead to a conviction.

Waldvogel is currently being tried again in Switzerland for unlawful sexual contact with children. The Swiss authorities would also like to clarify the position in connection with the sentence pronounced against him in Sri Lanka, as to whether this is enforceable in Switzerland. In order for this to happen, the Swiss authorities would require an official request for legal assistance and a formal decision of the Court and all the documents concerning this case from Sri Lanka. The Swiss Embassy in Colombo even offered to translate the documents relating to the trial at its own expense. Indeed, the whole question of whether Waldvogel could stand a new trial in Switzerland, while he has still not served the sentence he received *in absentia* in Sri Lanka, remains unclear.

NGOs in both Sri Lanka and Switzerland (ECPAT Switzerland), by contrast, communicated openly with each other, and sought to put pressure on Sri Lanka both to accelerate proceedings and to transmit information to Switzerland. ECPAT Switzerland informed the Swiss authorities when Waldvogel returned to Switzerland. In July 1998, the same organization wrote to the lawyer of PEACE, stressing the formalities that needed to be observed before the Sri Lankan sentence could be executed in Switzerland.

For a foreign verdict to be carried out in Switzerland, it must be a crime in both countries. The provisions for sexual offences must be equivalent. Such a verdict can be executed only if the executing state makes a formal application for legal assistance to Switzerland in one of its official languages (German, French or Italian). The sentence will be imposed up to the maximum possible for an equivalent offence. The foreign state must also guarantee that an offender will not be prosecuted again for the same offence if the sentence is served in Switzerland.

Pfister also committed a second crime. In November 1996, he was arrested and charged with committing bodily harm, together with a 36-year-old Belgian, who had been accused of paedophilia in Sri Lanka. Both men had gone to a guest-house and assaulted the wife and employees of the hotel manager. This was intended as a warning that they should not testify against the Belgian, who had been caught by the police when he was in the act of abusing two boys in the hotel in September 1996. It is believed that the two boys were the same ones whom Pfister and Waldvogel had abused in 1995. According to a number of newspaper articles, Pfister was arrested once more on 19 October 1998 for having abused yet again the same two Sri Lankan boys, who are now aged 16. The *Sunday Leader* newspaper of 7 March 1999 reported that Pfister had been released by a general amnesty and had fled Sri Lanka and returned to Switzerland.

Waldvogel is known to have travelled regularly to Sri Lanka on holiday since 1994. He also visited Thailand. Pfister, whose profession is not known, had lived in Sri Lanka for some time, and owned several apartments there. He often invited boys to these apartments and used them sexually. He also arranged for foreign guests to join him, and children were made available to them for sexual purposes. It could not be established whether he profited financially from these activities. Waldvogel was one of these 'guests'.

The case was widely discussed in Sri Lanka, because Pfister and Waldvogel were among the first foreigners to be arrested and convicted there for the sexual exploitation of children. They were not in fact the first, as the media stated – in 1995 a Canadian national had been convicted. After the verdict, the senior police officer conducting the investigation said he thought foreigners who offended against children should be extradited to their own country, so that they could be prosecuted according to their own national law. The Sri Lankan NGO involved in the case, on the other hand, expressed the opinion that foreigners should be sentenced in Sri Lanka, in order to make it clear there that sex with children is a crime.

Of the victims, the reports say, that 'the two boys seem to be street-children'. Their fate did arouse some interest, both within Sri Lanka and abroad, since they were themselves arrested under a statute dating from the time of the British Raj, which prohibits 'homosexual behaviour'. The boys were defended by a lawyer paid for by Pfister. Indeed, the boys were 'sentenced' for homosexuality, according to the Sri Lankan Penal Code. This law, which criminalized the acts of victims, has now been changed. They were ordered to remain in an 'educational home' until the age of 18. They escaped from this institution shortly afterwards. It is a measure of the work that requires to be done in this area that the boys were 'sentenced' before the offenders.

The only positive outcome of this sorry story is that the issue of sexual and commercial exploitation of children in Sri Lanka was brought to the attention of the public. The Sri Lankan police were also more active in this case (in contrast to the events surrounding Berger; see case history 5), and arrested the offenders at the scene of their crime. According to Naranjan, he lived in the Holiday Home, where the arrrests took place. The police said they picked him up on the streets of Colombo, near the Mount Lavinia crossing. Mullu said only that he lived in Colombo. Their educational status is unknown. Niranjan stated that his father was dead, the whereabouts of his mother unknown. No details are available on the origins or background of Mullu. It is clear that the authorities in Sri Lanka had no programme for the reintegration of abused children into society, and that the victims were themselves stigmatized and more or less left to their fate. There was no question of compensation.

The criminal law for sexual offences in Sri Lanka was amended in October 1995. Indeed, revision of the law was taking place during the investigation, and the issue was under public discussion at the time. Minors below the age of 18 are protected by a number of articles that punish the sexual exploitation of children. Homosexuality remains a crime. There is a historic irony in the fact that the British introduced the law in the first place, but subsequently saw fit to abolish it in their own country. The Indian sub-continent retains this colonial archaism. While Sri Lanka has amended its law protecting children, it still exposes them to punishment for 'acts against the order of nature'. Such anomalies, and the confusion arising from past imperial domination, need to be addressed.

8

Reign of Terror in Iloilo

Paul Maurer: Switzerland/the Philippines

In the summer of 1998, the public prosecutor of the Canton of Basle indicted a 35-year-old plumber, charging him with having had unlawful sexual contact with 20 Filipino children, aged between 9 and 19, between 1990 and 1996. It was in the 1980s, when he was on a trip to the United States, that Maurer met a Filipina woman who invited him to visit her in the Philippines. He went there for the first time in 1988. From the remote island of Panay, he visited the town of S. close to Iloilo. This place was virtually unknown to tourists. He evidently found life there so agreeable that from that time he travelled annually to S., spending several months there. He usually stayed with families whose trust he had won and on whom he lavished big presents. He gained their confidence and came to be seen by some as a member of the family.

In 1992, Maurer started to build his own house. When it was finished, he spent six months of every year there. The families in the town had complete trust in him, since they regularly left their sons to stay with him overnight. These families were very poor, and were appreciative of Maurer's gifts, which helped them to raise their standards of living to a degree that would otherwise have been impossible for them. He exploited the innocence of the victims' families, most of whom scarcely knew that sexual exploitation of children existed.

Maurer knew how to attract children. He was generous, offering toys, clothes, food and money. He organized camping trips for them. He was himself a highly organized person, and he kept lists of all the gifts he had given, including details of the sizes of clothing particular children had received. He also kept a record of the times when each boy was due to come to his house in order to perform sexual acts upon him. Maurer had a system of awarding points to boys who appeared on time, and he gave additional presents and money and further outings to those who had accumulated a certain number of points. Boys who did not put in an appearance at the specified time received 'penalty' points.

Maurer not only encouraged the boys to comply with his demands by offering rewards, he also intimidated them by threatening them with instruments of coercion – devices with which he could deliver electric shocks or paralyse them. He owned a number of weapons, including a 9 mm pistol and a 44 magnum Desert Eagle, which he had taken with him to the Philippines. The boys submitted to the man's sexual demands because they were afraid of him. They were obliged to take part in a variety of sexual acts. Maurer took pictures of them during these sexual activities, and regularly made them watch pornographic films. Sometimes he laid his guns on the table while he was sexually abusing the boys.

The people of the town were dismayed when, in 1996, they discovered that Maurer had sexually exploited the sons of so many families over such a long period. His offences came to light only when a number of victims had confided in someone close to them. This took place in May 1996. Their confidant was Kelsey, a young man who worked as a domestic servant for the accused, described as a 'friend and helper' of Maurer. When this young man learned from the victims what Maurer was doing, he could scarcely believe it. He confronted him with the stories, but Maurer brushed them aside, and said that some of the children were jealous since they had received no money from him.

Kelsey then made his own enquiries. He crept into Maurer's house at night with several friends, and witnessed the abuse that was regularly occurring. Kelsey ordered his three brothers – who were also associating with Maurer – to have nothing further to do with him. He told his own parents and an aunt what had happened. They did not believe him, and Kelsey was himself too frightened to go to the police. He asked a cousin, a doctor, to go with him to a social worker from the Department of Social Welfare and Development. She travelled to the village in order to question some of the children involved. They were too intimidated to tell her anything, and it was at this moment that Maurer was warned by two of his victims that someone from the Department was asking questions of the children with whom he had associated. He quickly packed his belongings and prepared to leave the country. The day before his flight (6 June 1996), he was seen burning video-cassettes in his garden.

In his haste, he overlooked a pile of documents, including letters from his family and friends in Europe. He also left records of his activities with the children. Some pornography was found, along with photographs he had taken of the children in a number of sexual positions.

It required both commitment and tenacity on the part of individuals – journalists, social workers, the state welfare office and ECPAT Philippines – before action was taken, and charges were formally brought against Maurer. The local police were informed of the accusations against him by the Department of Social Welfare, but they were reluctant to take action for two reasons: they had never experienced a case of sexual exploitation of children, and they were unwilling to offend a guest in their country. There was, in any case, still no legal deposition. This was not made until 13 September 1996, when two of the victims, accompanied by parents and a Social Welfare Department social worker, went to the 2nd Municipal Circuit Trial Court S – San Remegio and Delision. The judge issued two arrest warrants, and set bail at 30,000 pesos (US$960) for both cases. In the Philippines, Maurer was charged with contravention of article III of the Republic Act 7610 (child prostitution and other sexual abuse). The police were unable to execute the arrest warrant, since Maurer had fled and his whereabouts were unknown. The judge therefore decided to dismiss the case.

In November 1996, a Filipino journalist, Romel Bagares, many of whose relatives live in S., wrote a three-part report on the case for the *Philippine Star*. As a result, Senator Ernesto Herrera, in another newspaper article, challenged the police and the customs authorities to start a national manhunt for Maurer. The senator revealed that a 12-year-old victim of Maurer had recently died of an undiagnosed disease. It was feared that Maurer might have been HIV-positive and transmitted the virus to his victims. A subsequent medical examination carried out in Switzerland proved negative. It was as a result of this anxiety over the possible risk of infection to the victims that ECPAT Philippines became involved in the case. In March 1997, ECPAT sent the information in its possession to ECPAT Switzerland, who passed it on to the Federal Police Department there. Cooperation between ECPAT Switzerland and ECPAT Philippines was very effective – indeed, the public prosecutor acknowledged that without the support of NGOs, the investigations would never have been brought to such a satisfactory conclusion. The Swiss Embassy in Manila was also extremely helpful in facilitating communication. The Basle public prosecutor made use of both official and unofficial channels in pursuing the investigation, and the Basle authorities expended a great deal of time, energy and resources on the case. After using ECPAT Switzerland as an intermediary at first, ECPAT Philippines developed direct communication with the public prosecutor.

ECPAT Switzerland played a significant part in supporting the investigation. Among other things, it served as a channel of communication between NGOs in the country of the offence and the investigating authorities in Switzerland. It kept those NGOs informed about the legal principles and procedures in Switzerland, and pressed them to speed up the flow of information. It served also as a cultural intermediary, helping to build up confidence in the Swiss authorities.

The details concerning the allegations were passed on from the Federal Police Department in Switzerland to the Basle city authorities, in whose jurisdiction Maurer was living. As part of the Basle public prosecutor's enquiries, Maurer's telephone was tapped. In October 1997, shortly before Maurer was due to return to the Philippines, he was arrested. In November 1997, two investigators from the public prosecutor's office went to the Philippines, and spent several weeks interviewing witnesses and victims. Evidence was sent from the Philippines to Switzerland. In summer 1998, Maurer was formally charged with multiple sexual acts with the childen, sexual coercion, pornography and attempted coercion (articles 187 of the Swiss Criminal Code – sexual acts with children; 189 – sexual coercion; 197 – pornography; 181 – general coercion; and 68 – multiple acts). The maximum sentence in the Philippines would have been 30 years' imprisonment. In Switzerland the maximum is 15 years for the same offences. The double criminality rule applies, but, as in the case of Berger, under the principle of *lex mitior*, the Swiss sentencing practice applies.

According to charges brought by the public prosecutor, it was alleged that during Maurer's stay in S., the children and young people were compelled to masturbate the accused, to masturbate each other and to be photographed while they were doing so. On one occasion he is alleged to have forced one of the victims to perform anal intercourse on him, and he tried to do the same to the boy. He regularly showed the boys a pornographic film, and at the same time showed them books that displayed sexual acts between men and women, between men and other men, and between people and animals. He was also charged with using physical force against some of the boys, in order to weaken and break their resistance to him. He gained their compliance by showing them a device that could administer electric shocks. The boys were said to have feared punishment, and to have been unable to escape from Maurer, either because the house was locked, or because they did not have sufficient physical strength to protect themselves.

Maurer is described as coming from a decent background, having grown up in a typical Swiss middle-class family. Until his arrest in October 1997, he lived in the room he had occupied since childhood in his parents' house. He owned several weapons, and was known to be obsessive about guns and weapons. During his time in the Philippines, he drove to a shooting-stand each week for firearms practice.

The victims are said to come from families who are poor and live in difficult conditions. The circumstances of three brothers who were all victims of Maurer were summed up in the *Philippine Star*:

> The brothers live alone with their mother. The family lives in a grass hut on land belonging to the mother's parents-in-law. When it rains, the yard turns into a sea of mud. Her husband is a farm labourer on the farm of an acquaintance, and receives ten per cent of the crop harvested by him. Some of the parents involved did not want to speak about what happened to their sons, as they considered that Maurer could not be so bad, since he had given the children many presents (money, clothing, toys and food).
>
> Maurer lent money to the families of children who were faithful to him. Neighbours told how children on the way to school queued up at Maurer's holiday home to receive 'baon' (pocket money). 1989 saw the start of annual trips to Boracay Island, Puerta Princessa Palawan and even Coronacal in South Cotabato. Up to eight children at a time went on these expeditions, which lasted as long as a week. Maurer kept precise records of everything which he bought for the children.

The witnesses were interviewed in the Philippines, in the presence of two Swiss criminal investigators, two policemen from the Iloilo Police Department, a female social worker from the Department of Social Welfare, and a female translator. The first witness was reluctant to speak, because he feared he would have to travel to Switzerland to make statements. Only when his employer – a retired judge for whom he is now working as a domestic servant – reassured him was he willing to speak. These interviews provided sufficient evidence for the trial in Switzerland, and removed the need for the children to leave their country in order to give evidence. The interviews were transmitted to the accused each day by fax for his reaction. No confrontation between the accused and his victims was necessary.

The offences were committed between 1990 and 1996. The case was taken up in the Philippines in 1996, and investigations began in Switzerland late in 1996. There is no question of compensation, since only victims against whom crimes are committed in Switzerland can be compensated.

The trial took place in the Criminal Court of Basle in the early summer of 1999, and on 9 June Maurer was convicted of having sexually abused at least thirteen children in the Philippines between 1989 and 1996. He was sentenced to six years in prison. The sentence was commuted to at least an equivalent period in a closed psychiatric hospital. He will undergo treatment until such time as he is considered capable of living in the community without abusing children.

This was the first extraterritorial trial in Basle, and the first in Switzerland involving Filipino victims. The sentencing took into consideration not only the sexual abuse of the children, but also the creation of pornography and the psychological intimidation Maurer had deployed to make the children comply with his wishes.

In her judgment, the president of the Court, Mrs Lenzinger, drew attention to the extent to which Maurer had abused the trust of the children and their families. As a well-to-do white man, he had appeared to offer them gifts and opportunities – such as payment of school fees – that they could otherwise never have expected. Maurer accepted the decision of the Court and did not appeal against it.

Editor's Note

Certain patterns establish themselves. The enormous social gulf between the offender and the children he abuses – almost as though deliberately seeking out the most innocent, least aware people who may be the more easily duped into believing in his benevolence. The compulsive tendency of the abuser to record, take pictures and videos of his actions, possibly to relive them in fantasy, or perhaps simply using the technology as a substitute for memory. But this recurs with sufficient frequency to be remarkable. The unwillingness of the people who benefit from his largess to believe the worst – even the collusion of some of the abused children who warned him to escape before the net closed in on him – recurs in several cases. There is, in this, another metaphor for the relationship between rich and poor in the world: dependency, an unwillingness to disturb even pathological structures, when maintenance of the status quo seems to promise more than fundamental change.

9

The Silence of the Authorities

Marcel Thierry: France/Thailand

Marcel Thierry, a 45-year-old journalist, was arrested and convicted of sexually abusing two Thai boys in Thailand in November 1993. The Court of First Instance in Bangkok found that Thierry had violated the Thai Criminal Code (Section 279, title IX), by committing indecent acts on children under the age of 15, having performed oral sex with them. He was also convicted of corrupting minors. (Section 279 says that 'whoever commits an indecent act on a child under fifteen years of age, whether such a child consents or not, shall be punished with imprisonment not exceeding ten years or fine not exceeding 20,000 baht, or both'.) At that time, sexual intercourse was punishable only when it involved girls. As far as boys were concerned, only 'indecent acts' against them were punishable under Thai law. This anomaly has since been corrected.

The Thai tourist police arrested Thierry on 5 November 1993 in his room at the King's Mansion Hotel in Bangkok. They found a 14-year-old boy naked in his bed. The search and arrest took place following a tip-off from the Committee for the Protection of Children's Rights (CPCR) in Thailand. This NGO had been contacted by a woman who worked at the centre for street-children where one of the boys was then living. This employee of the centre said that a second boy, a 13-year-old who lived there, had told staff that Thierry had promised him 100 baht (US$2.50) if he would pose naked. The boy had in fact been sexually abused by Thierry and had escaped, taking the man's camera with him. The film inside the stolen camera was developed and photographs of naked children were found. This boy then led the police to Thierry's room, where he was found with the 14-year-old.

Thierry denied having sexual contact with the boys. He claimed that he had taken pity on them because they were street-children, and had, out of charity, offered them a place to stay in his hotel room. After he had been arrested and brought before the Court of First Instance, Thierry was granted bail in the sum of 200,000 baht (US$5,000). At the same time, the French Embassy requested Thierry's passport from the Thai authorities. The Embassy then returned the passport to him. The subsequent explanation of the Embassy was that he had needed his passport in order to withdraw money from the bank.

The Bangkok Court convicted Thierry and sentenced him to four years' imprisonment. Thierry appealed against the judgment. Pending the outcome of the appeal, the Court again granted bail, on payment of a surety of 300,000 baht (US$7,500). Within a few days Thierry had left Thailand. Officials at the French Embassy denied that they were responsible for the fact that he had escaped Thai jurisdiction, on the grounds that the visa entitling him to stay in Thailand had expired by the time his passport had been returned to him. The implication is that the onus was upon the Thai authorities to prevent him from leaving the country. Almost a year later, the Thai Court of Appeal upheld the conviction and sentence.

Thierry is presumed to have returned to France, where, although his conduct appears to violate French criminal law, which prohibits sexual contact abroad with minors under the age of 15 and the corruption of minors abroad, he has not been charged. Prosecution remains a possibility. The French authorities could have prosecuted (but were not required to do so) under the legislation in force at the time of the offence (1993), subject to two conditions. First, the act committed must be an offence both in France and in the country where it was committed. This requirement clearly was fulfilled. Second, there must be a formal complaint by the relevant authorities, or by the victim. No formal complaint was filed. This requirement was removed in June 1998, and this means that Thierry could still be prosecuted in France.

Although the offences took place six years ago, the usual three-year limit for prosecution has not yet expired, since prosecution in Thailand stopped time from running. In the same way, the 'double jeopardy' principle, which prevents an offender from being prosecuted twice for the same offence, does not rule out a prosecution in France, since Thierry did not fully serve his sentence in Thailand.

All that is known about Thierry is that he is a single man working as a journalist. The information available on the background of the victims is slight. One boy is stated to be 'probably' an orphan, aged 13, and the other one 'has a family'. The 13-year-old is taken care of by a street-children protection centre.

The story demonstrates a lack of cooperation between the French and Thai authorities, and possibly an unfamiliarity with the extraterritorial provisions on the part of those concerned in both jurisdictions. Reluctance to incur the costs involved in extraterritorial prosecutions may also be an element.

This case was seen as a challenge to the efficacy of the extraterritorial prosecution of sexual tourists. It demonstrated to those working in the field that if an offender could escape from the country in which the offence had been committed, there was no certainty that he would be subject to prosecution in his home country. In this case, the *legal* obstacle to prosecution appears to have been the absence of retroactivity in the French so-called extraterritorial law, which was enacted in 1994 – so-called because the concept of extraterritoriality has existed in French penal law since 1866, whereby the law is applicable to all crimes (*crimes*) committed by a French national outside the territory of the republic, and to misdemeanours (*délits*), if these are also punishable by the law of the country where they were committed. A complaint by the victim or by the authorities of the country where the misdemeanour has occurred must also be made.

The law of 1994 did not actually create a new offence punishable under French law, but created a new aggravating circumstance for an existing one. 'If an adult engages in sexual conduct, without violence, threat or surprise, with a person under 15, this shall be punished with imprisonment of two years and a fine of FF 200,000' was the existing offence: the new aggravating circumstance applies when this sexual conduct is accompanied by payment. The offender now risks imprisonment for ten years and a fine of FF 1,000,000. The objective of this was to combat commercial sexual exploitation of children, and it applied to French nationals, both within France and outside. It was aimed specifically at the *délit* of sexual tourism. The 1994 law also removed the need for double criminality and prior complaint by the victim. Doubt remained that offences committed before the enactment of this law would be affected by it. It was widely believed that offences committed against minors abroad by a French national before 1994 could not be punished.

A number of features published in the press confirmed this perception.

While it is true that these conditions might have hindered the prosecution in France of the Thierry case prior to 1994, there already existed other provisions in the French Criminal Code that could have been invoked: under article 331, an attack on the modesty of minors under 15 is punishable with imprisonment from three to five years and a fine of FF 6,000 to FF 60,000; under articles 334(2), corruption of a minor under 16 is punishable with imprisonment for between two and ten years, and a fine of FF 100,000 to FF 1,000,000; under articles 283 and 286, child pornography (*outrage aux bonnes moeurs*) is punishable.

In June 1998, the French Parliament passed a law removing the requirements of double criminality and prior denunciation (either by the victim or by the state in which the offence was committed) from all cases of sexual offences against minors, including corruption of minors and child pornography. These simplifications should also be applicable to offences committed before the passing of the 1994 amendments.

Furthermore, an NGO could act as *parti civil* to claim compensation for the victim of sexual offences, if the NGO has been in existence for more than five years at the time of the crime, if its purpose includes combating sexual violence or the ill-treatment of children, and if the prosecution was initiated by the victim (or his or her legal guardian) or by the Ministère Public (the prosecuting authorities.) A French NGO could start the case even without the authorization of the victims. (Whether a foreign NGO could do so is not clear). Problems with language and translation, the uncertainty over whether extraterritorial legislation is applicable in the case, and the lack of precedents on procedure may deter an NGO from doing so.

When a *délit* is concerned, the period of limitation expires three years after the offence was committed. However, prosecutions brought by the competent foreign authorities stop time from running, as long as they were brought within the time stipulated by Thai law. This means that although the offence occurred six years ago, a prosecution begun in Thailand does not prevent prosecution in France.

This case was raised during the Stockholm Congress by a Thai prosecutor, who stated that the absence of retroactivity of extraterritorial laws could cause prosecutions to fail. At the same time, a Thai NGO, FACE, and a French NGO, Juristes du Monde, made common cause to work together to ensure that a prosecution would be possible in France.

This case, more than most, demonstrates the difficulties faced by those campaigning, particularly in the early 1990s, for the principle of extraterritoriality in child sex abuse cases. Indeed, it was precisely the inability of the authorities to pursue such offenders that has now led to the enactment of such legislation in most countries, the clarification of existing legislation, and a closer definition of child sex tourism.

10

A Network of Corruption

The Draguignan Case: France/Romania

This case involved seven men convicted in October 1997 by the Tribunal de Grande Instance in Draguignan of sexual offences against children in both France and Romania. Investigations into the affair began in the summer of 1994 in the south of France. They followed complaints from some travelling fairground entertainers in St Tropez that Laurent Deneuve, a 29-year-old seasonal worker, had raped and sexually abused young children. During the search of a priest's house near Lyon, where Deneuve was staying, the police found pornographic photographs of children, together with addresses. Deneuve admitted that he was a paedophile and was living with a 14-year-old child. He also confessed that he had been to Romania and Thailand several times to have sexual contact with children. He revealed that on at least one occasion in 1994, he had visited Romania with Horace Creuset, a 70-year-old Frenchman. Deneuve had also had sexual contact with a 14-year-old child in Romania – child C. – and had placed him in an orphanage in Bucharest, where he visited him.

Police then contacted Creuset, and interviewed him in October 1994. During a search of his house, child pornography was also discovered, including some material designed for French-speaking paedophiles that had been sent by a Belgian living in Thailand. Creuset admitted that in 1994 he had paid for sexual relations with minors abroad. He insisted, however, that they had all been over the age of 15, and that therefore he had not violated the relevant parts of the Criminal Code.

Their questioning of Creuset led the police to Jean Bouvier, a 40-year-old who was living in the same house. Bouvier denied he was a paedophile, although he admitted to an interest in pornographic videos showing the rape of children. He also claimed that Creuset had provided information to a group of paedophiles that enabled them to make contact, for sexual purposes, with children in Romania.

Julien Lavoine, a 33-year-old from Lyon, was also an associate of Creuset. They had visited Romania together in 1994 and 1995. The police questioned him in January 1996, and Lavoine confessed to having abused a certain child N. in Romania. He asserted, however – like Creuset – that the child was over the age of 15, and that he had in consequence not been in violation of the relevant article of the Criminal Code. Lavoine also admitted that he had organized the entry of two Romanian children – N. and B. – to France. He had also abused child N. in France, but denied that he had abused child B., who had been entrusted to him by child B.'s parents.

The other three offenders were Antoine Barrière, Serge Galien and David Daladier. These had all provided accommodation for the children N. and B., the former two near Paris, and Daladier near Lyon. Barrière, who is the son of a senior official at the Paris Court, had also been in contact with the offender Bouvier, to whom he had sent a number of videos of child pornography. Barrière was interrogated in March 1996.

Galien, who was 35, also admitted that he had sheltered the two children, but denied any sexual contact with them. Although the police found photographs of him together with child N., Galien protested that they had merely mimed the sex act. He insisted that he was not a paedophile. It later emerged that he had worked with journalists for a television report on paedophilia. He had acted as a guide to the journalists as they were making the film. Although his face had been blanked out of the TV pictures, he was recognized by one of the investigating officers who had earlier questioned him.

In August 1996, child N. was located in a squat in a Paris suburb. He stated that he had known Creuset and Lavoine in Romania, and that he had been brought by them to France. He had had sexual contact with Lavoine, Barrière and Galien. Child N. was placed in a children's home, from where he is said to have 'escaped' several days later. He was not present at the trial.

Finally, police interviewed the 37-year-old Daladier in January 1997. They had found photographs of him with child B. and child N. He was known to them by his first name. The full identity of Daladier was later revealed by child B., who, during an interview with the Belgian police in Liège, told them that he wished to join his adoptive father, Daladier, near Lyon.

In order to convict Deneuve, Creuset and Lavoine under the relevant section of the Criminal Code (article 227.26.4), the Court had to find that the children they admitted to having abused were under the age of 15 when the unlawful sexual contact took place. In the case of child N., abused by Creuset and Lavoine, a medical examination had taken place before he absconded from the children's home. This established that his bone age was 15, and confirmed his own statement that he had been under 15 when the abuse took place. On the basis of this evidence, the Court rejected the claims of Creuset and Lavoine that child N. had been 15 at that time. When it came to determining the age of child N. at the time of the offences, the Court rejected a birth certificate produced by the defence, which did not show any photograph of the victim.

In convicting Deneuve, Creuset and Lavoine, the Court did not follow the usual step, which would have been to send an international rogatory commission to Romania. It found that the confessions of the men involved, the visas on their passports, and the testimony of child N. provided sufficient evidence. In Romania, sexual abuse of girls under the age of 14 is an offence. Romanian law also penalizes sexual relations between persons of the same sex if committed in public; an adult having sexual relations with a minor of the same sex is liable to a term of two to seven years' imprisonment.

Police suspected the existence of a wider network of paedophiles, whose members have also abused children N. and B. A second investigation into this is still going on. A parallel investigation was also carried out in Thailand, in order to confirm information about a Belgian who had sent pornographic material which was found in the houses of several of the offenders. This inquiry proved unsuccessful.

Laurent Deneuve, 29 at the time of the offences, was born in the north of France, and is described as a 'seasonal worker' at festivals, ski resorts and so on. He is stated to have had one previous conviction for 'immoral behaviour'. Horace Creuset, 70, retired, was said to have had one earlier conviction for immoral behaviour, and to be in 'rather low living standards'. Jean Bouvier was 40, of unknown occupation, with no criminal record, and of 'unknown' social circumstances. Julien Lavoine, 33, from Lyon, was a restaurant and hotel worker, single, with one conviction for 'immoral behaviour'. Antoine Barrière was 23, living in Paris, a chauffeur by occupation, and the son of a senior official at the Tribunal de Grande Instance of Paris. Serge Galien was 36, single, living in the suburbs of

Paris, an 'executive', whose social circumstances were 'good'. David Daladier was 37, employed by S.N.C.F., the French railway company. He was single, his circumstances 'unknown'. Of the victims, child N. was 13 or 15 at the time of the offences. Born in Romania, in Negresti Oas, he lives in a squat in the suburbs of Paris. Nothing is known of his occupation or social circumstances. Child B. was 'younger than thirteen and a half at the time of the offences against him'. His place of birth, residence, education and social circumstances are all unknown.

This was the first case (October 1997) tried under the 1994 law. A few months earlier, in the summer of 1997, a number of investigations had taken place in France in relation to possession of child pornography. Several of the individuals under investigation had committed suicide. The press had alleged that a 'witch-hunt' was taking place, and this made it a sensitive issue. These suicides led to the dropping of a proposal by the then French government intended to criminalize the mere possession of child pornography.

The Court of First Instance consists of a president and two judges. This correctional court can deal with all *délits* that are subject to a penalty of imprisonment or a fine equal to or exceeding FF 25,000. There is no jury, but any decision is subject to an appeal.

The accused were charged thus: Deneuve, Creuset and Lavoine with sexual abuse of minors under the age of 15 with payment, in France and abroad, and in Romania, with receipt of paedophile video-cassettes in an organized network, this having originated from the criminal act of making, recording or transmitting child pornography with intent to distribute; Barrière with sexual abuse of children under the age of 15 with payment in France, and receipt of paedophile video-cassettes; Galien with corruption of a minor under the age of 15, and sexual abuse of children under the age of 15 with payment in France; Daladier with sexual abuse of children and receipt of cassettes.

The articles of the French Criminal Code that the defendants were accused of violating were article 227-22, corruption of minors; article 227-23, making, with intent to distribute, pornographic images involving minors; articles 227 and 227-26.4, sexual conduct on a minor under 15, without violence, threat or surprise, committed in France and abroad and with payment; article 321-1, receipt of the proceeds of crime; articles 321-2 and 321-2.2, receipt as an organized network; articles 227-29, 321-3, 321-9, 321-10 and 321-11, additional penalties.

Evidence was obtained through interviews with the accused, the statements of a number of witnesses and the seizure of documents at the homes of the offenders. Confiscated pornographic videos and photographs were also shown during the hearing. Arguments made in defence included the ages of the children, and the claim that gifts, not payments, were made to them. One of the accused claimed only to have mimed the sex act with one of the children. They argued that they had not acted in concert. They protested that NGOs were not entitled to be heard in the case. The victims were not present in the court. Child N. was questioned during the inquiry, but then fled.

The sentences were severe. Deneuve was sentenced to 10 years' imprisonment, with 5 years' deprivation of civic and civil rights; Creuset to 15 years, and 5 years' deprivation of rights; Bouvier to 5 years, of which 3 were suspended on condition of good behaviour; Lavoine to 10 years, with 5 years' deprivation of rights; Barrière to 6 years and 5 years' deprivation of rights; Galien to 6 years and 5 years' deprivation of rights; and Daladier to 7 years and 5 years' deprivation of rights. Deneuve, Creuset and Lavoine all had previous convictions for sexual offences. All the accused appealed, except Bouvier. On appeal, in November 1998, the penalties were slightly modified, mostly in the form of sentences reduced by a year. All are currently in jail. There is no compulsory treatment during their period of detention.

The severity of the sentences may reflect the fact that this was the first time the Court had applied the law of 1994, and there may have been an element of setting a precedent and making an example of the offenders. The five-year sentence imposed on Bouvier, who had not abused any children but had only handled child pornography as part of an organized group, was noteworthy, as was the 15 years imposed on Creuset, who had offended before. The Court stressed the cruelty of the paedophile network, the more so since when extracts from the seized videos were shown, these were so shocking that the president of the Court moved quickly to put an end to the viewing. This case attracted considerable media attention, principally because it was the first time the 1994 law had been applied, and because it involved the dismantling of a countrywide paedophile network. The Association against Child Prostitution (ACPE) played an active role in publicizing the case.

The victim of a criminal offence may be awarded damages, and French law allows an NGO to represent the public interest in cases of sexual offences against children (see case history 8). In this instance, two organizations served this role: the Association against Child Prostitution and Action against Prostitution. Their presence was opposed by the defence. Action against Prostitution was excluded by the tribunal, since it was unable to show defence of children as one of its objectives.

The period between the time of the first complaint in St Tropez and the final judgment from the Draguignan Court of Appeal spanned four years. A law dealing with prevention and punishment of sexual offences against children was adopted in June 1998. Among other things, convicted persons may be compelled to stay away from places frequented by children, prohibited from employment or any activity that involves contact with children, and must undergo compulsory treatment. Failure to observe an order can lead to imprisonment.

The import or export of child pornography is now punishable. The meaning of child pornography has been extended, and penalties for sexual abuse of a child under 15 have been increased. The application of extraterritorial jurisdiction has been simplified (removal of double criminality and prior complaint now extends to a number of other sexual offences against children).

Legal entities can be made criminally responsible for certain sexual offences against children. It has been made easier for organizations to represent the public interest in cases of such offences. The period of limitation does not begin to run until the age of majority of the victim. If no prosecution is pursued, the public prosecutor must give reasons in writing. Child victims may have to undergo a medico-psychological examination to assess their needs. Evidence may be taken from child victims by audio-visual means, and they may be accompanied by psychologist, doctor or member of their family. A national databank has been set up of DNA profiles of those convicted of abuse of children.

11

The Teacher and the Thai Boy

Marc Boonen: Belgium/Thailand

On 18 May 1998, the Correctional Tribunal in Bruges convicted Marc Boonen, a 48-year-old unmarried teacher, of unlawful sexual contact with a child aged under 16 years in Thailand. This was the second conviction of a Belgian national for sex tourism, and the first one under the new extraterritorial law of 1995. Boonen was arrested early in the evening of 16 July 1996 in a hotel room in Pattaya with a 14-year-old boy. Both were naked. Boonen had arrived in Thailand two weeks earlier. He had met the victim several days before his arrest. He had bought clothes for him, and invited him to his hotel room to take a shower and then to watch television.

Yongrut, the victim, was strolling in the Royal Garden Shopping Centre in Pattaya on the afternoon of 16 July. There he met Boonen, who speaks a little Thai, and who suggested to the boy that he accompany him around the centre. At about 5.20, Boonen asked the boy to follow him to his hotel room at the White Inn Hotel. When they reached the room, Boonen undressed, asked the boy to do the same, and then told him to masturbate him. He had promised to give the boy 300 baht (US$12). At this moment, there was a knock at the door. Boonen opened it, and was confronted by a police officer, who came into the room, followed by others. The situation was obvious. The police took photographs and held Boonen in custody. On that day, he admitted to the Thai police that he had told the victim to follow him to his hotel room. The police said they had seen him approach a group of young boys. They observed that, after negotiating with them, he took one of them to his hotel.

After three days, he was released on bail of US$20,000. This sum was collected from friends of the offender, a Canadian, a Frenchman and two Dutch people, and delivered to the police by a Thai national. Boonen had asked the Belgian Embassy in Bangkok for help, but was told that nothing could be done to assist him. Although his passport had been confiscated, Boonen managed to leave Thailand on 8 August 1996. He returned to Belgium via Amsterdam, entering the country by means of his identity card. A Belgian journalist who heard of the arrest in Thailand published an article in a Belgian newspaper. The Thai Embassy in Belgium translated this article and sent it to Thailand. It appeared that the authorities in Pattaya were reluctant to bring the case to court.

The Thai NGO FACE and ECPAT Belgium played an important role in this case by facilitating contacts between the two countries. ECPAT Belgium several times requested that the new extraterritorial legislation be applied vigorously. On 20 November 1996, the Belgian Department of Judicial Affairs, through the Belgian Embassy in Bangkok, officially asked the Thai authorities to help with their investigation. There was a lapse of six months before the relevant Thai laws and the dossier on Boonen were translated, and almost a year passed before practical steps were taken by the *juge d'instruction*. The delay in getting this case started remains difficult to account for. It is suggested that the horror surrounding the Dutroux affair (see below), a few weeks before this case, absorbed all the energies of the judicial authorities.

In June 1997, a year after his previous arrest, he returned to Thailand for a two-month stay. FACE subsequently informed the Thai authorities when Boonen had returned to Belgium. On 8 August 1997, the Belgian prosecutor asked the judicial authorities in Pattaya for assistance. The following month a delegation to Belgium from the Attorney-General's Office in Thailand played a decisive part. A few days before their arrival in Ghent to meet their Belgian counterparts, Boonen was arrested: by this time, it was September 1997. In his first statement in Belgium, he confessed that he had had unlawful sexual contact with the 14-year-old Thai boy. Before Boonen was prosecuted in Belgium, the judicial authorities obtained an assurance that proceedings would be stopped in Thailand, on the principle that no one should be tried twice for the same crime (*ne bis in idem*).

The media took a lively interest in the case. Following the publicity it received, Boonen engaged a lawyer and subsequently changed his story. He now said the victim had come of his own accord to the hotel room, and that it was he who had initiated the sexual contact. He also denied what he had previously admitted, namely, that he had had earlier sexual contact with the boy between 30 June and 16 July 1996. He now claimed the boy knew the number of his room because he had met him two days earlier and taken him there, but he denied any sexual contact with him on that occasion.

Boonen appeared before the Correctional Tribunal. This Court of First Instance has no jury. He was charged under articles 372, 379 and 382 *bis* of the Belgium Criminal Code, namely, attack on the modesty of a person, or with the help of a person under the age of 18; corruption of a person under the age of 18 for the sexual gratification of others; and prohibition of someone who poses a real danger of repeating a paedophile offence from contact with children and young people. The Court found that Boonen had violated articles 372 and 382 *bis*, but not article 379. The maximum sentence under article 372 would have been five years' imprisonment.

The pictures taken by the police in Pattaya were not, in themselves, sufficient proof of the offence, although they served as a *commencement de preuve*. The statement of the victim and the first statement of the offender when he was arrested in Belgium were accepted by the Court. The boy did not have to be present at the trial; he had been interviewed by the Thai police, *in camera*, for his own protection.

The defence of the accused was based upon the inapplicability of the extraterritorial law of April 1995. The defence claimed that masturbation is an attack on modesty committed with the help of a minor and not upon a minor. The defence also disputed article 379, saying that masturbation was not corruption for the sexual gratification of others. It was further claimed that the three days spent in custody in Thailand constituted a sentence, and that the unusually high level of bail represented a judicial arrangement with the Thai justice system. On these grounds, the defence invoked the double jeopardy principle. Moreover, since Boonen had been back to Thailand without any trouble, this was adduced as proof that he had already been judged in Thailand. The defence also sought to justify paedophilia abroad, saying that the values of the country where the acts were committed were different, and claiming that the child had not only provoked him, but had no doubt also been involved in many other commercial sexual transactions.

The offender was unmarried, described as a teacher, and was a respectable middle-class man. He had travelled to Thailand several times a year since 1992, as well as to Laos, Cambodia, Burma and the Philippines. He was a teacher of 10- to 14-year-olds. He also worked as an instructor in holiday camps for young people.

The victim was 14 when the offence was committed. He had no regular residence, but lived on the beach at Pattaya, and slept in a hotel when he had the resources to do so. He had left his home in Pichit province, where he was in theory attending school, and had travelled by train to Bangkok. After a few days there, he was placed in a shelter for street-children in Nonthaburi province, where he studied. He escaped (*sic*) the school in 1995, and arrived in Pattaya one week before the events described above. His social circumstances are briefly described as 'very bad'. His subsequent fate is tersely described as 'unknown'.

Boonen was sentenced to one year in prison, but the Court in Belgium required only a half of this sentence to be served. In addition, Boonen was banned from teaching for ten years, and his civil rights were withdrawn for a period of five years. It is stated that he has not been compelled to undergo any special treatment, 'except medical treatment for a nervous breakdown'.

A number of issues are highlighted by this case. The trial took place shortly after the infamous Dutroux case, in which the accused was found to have molested and murdered a number of children, and to have buried them in the grounds of houses where he had lived. It is impossible to exaggerate the effect this had on the psyche of the people of Belgium. The fact that an apparently respectable citizen could have perpetrated such crimes, and that there had been a cover-up by the authorities of their own neglect and indifference to a proper investigation of the events, shocked the country, and led to widespread public anguish and discussions about the nature of Belgian society. It may be that Boonen retracted his earlier confession for fear that he might be tainted by the prevailing hysteria and anger at the time of the Dutroux case.

There is a tacit recognition of this in the Boonen case, since this was only the second case in Belgium in which a Belgian national had been convicted for sex tourism, and was the first one to have been based on the new extraterritorial law of 13 April 1995. The one-year sentence may be regarded as lenient, since only six months of it actually had to be served.

In Belgium, the extraterritorial law specifically enacted to cover offences against minors was a response to the so-called 'Spartacus' case in November 1994. John Stamford, a British citizen, who had committed serious sexual offences against minors abroad, was arrested in Belgium. The Court refused to convict him on the basis of his abuse of children abroad (if he had been Belgian, he could have been convicted under the then existing extraterritorial law). He was convicted only for the less serious offence of distributing obscene publications (*diffusion d'écrits contraires aux bonnes moeurs*). The law of April 1995 allows the authorities to prosecute anyone in Belgium (whether Belgian or not) who has committed any of the offences of articles 372, 373, 375, 376 and 377 of the Belgian Criminal Code, if the offence was against someone under 16. There is no need for a complaint or an official request from the country where the offences occurred.

The Centre of Equality of Opportunity and Opposition to Racism sought to become a representative of the public interest (*parti civil*) and asked for compensation on behalf of the victim and on behalf of itself (*dédommagement moral*). A declaration signed by the mother of the victim, authorizing the Centre to represent him, had been made after the sentence of the Court of First Instance had been passed; the Centre could not, therefore, represent the interests of the victim. The claim for compensation to the value of about US$15,000 was rejected. The Centre has appealed against this decision.

After the case, the minister of justice ordered the preparation of a new law concerning offences against minors. The draft of this law in December 1998 officially deletes the requirement of double criminality for the application of the extraterritorial law of April 1998. It also protects young persons up to the age of 18 from commercial sexual exploitation.

Both ECPAT Belgium and the Centre for Equality of Opportunity and Opposition to Racism (which is not an NGO) have made recommendations to amend the existing law:

• the description of the offence in the extraterritorial law (on the person under the age of 16) is not identical with that in article 372 of the Penal Code (on the person or with the help of the person under the age of 16);
• the restrictive conditions under which the interests of society may be represented: this is possible only when the offence of corruption of

minors and prostitution is established – which was designed to combat white slave trafficking;

- the requirement for double criminality in relation to minors (the draft of the new law does away with this requirement); and
- the age of protection should be raised to 18 years (this, too, is included in the same draft law).

12

The Escape of a Dangerous Man

Lode Claessens: Belgium/Sri Lanka

This case involves an investigation that is still in progress. It concerns Lode Claessens, a 36-year-old stevedore from the Antwerp region. He is accused of unlawful sexual contact with two 14-year-old boys in Sri Lanka. Although he was arrested and held in custody in Sri Lanka, no trial took place, since he escaped to Belgium. The case is before the prosecutor of the Antwerp Judicial District, and few further facts are known.

Claessens visited Sri Lanka twice a year from 1991 to 1996, each visit a stay of some weeks. He was usually met at Colombo airport by a Swiss friend, Anton Perlmann, who has lived in Sri Lanka since 1988, and who owns a guest-house there. The police suspected that this business was a cover, and that Perlmann's real purpose lay in procuring children for sex tourists. During one visit in 1996, Perlmann met Claessens at the airport, as he had been requested to do. He was accompanied by two 14-year-old boys. All four went by taxi to the Castle Hill hotel at the beach resort of Matara. Local NGOs had earlier alerted the hotel owner to their concern that boys were regularly being sexually abused there. When Perlmann, Claessens and the two boys reached their rooms, the owner called the local police. The police arrived shortly afterwards, and found Claessens and the two boys naked in their room. They arrested Claessens, and all three were imprisoned.

After 14 days, Claessens was released on bail. Together with Perlmann, he returned to the Castle Hill hotel, and made threats against the hotel owner, ordering him to withdraw his testimony. They then beat him up so badly that he required hospital treatment. Claessens and Perlmann were both arrested and imprisoned to await trial. The prosecutor asked the Court to postpone the trial, so that Claessens could also be charged with the additional offence of rape of a minor, as well as the attack on the hotel owner. Claessens then managed to escape, and went to the Netherlands, using a Swiss passport. He left that passport in Amsterdam, and proceeded to Belgium using his own identity card.

The proceedings in Sri Lanka came to an end when the file relating to Claessens was 'lost', possibly as the result of a bribe. The boys concerned, who had previously been arrested for similar offences, were placed in a protective shelter. In spite of this, Claessens still managed to visit them there after he had jumped bail, but before leaving the country – probably to persuade them to withdraw their testimony against him.

It is understood that the proceedings against Claessens are going forward in Belgium, based on information transmitted to the Belgian authorities by Interpol and the testimony of two witnesses in Sri Lanka. The Belgian police subsequently arrested Claessens for the quite separate offence of possessing Japanese child pornography.

13

A Culture Clash

Boris Bjorkmann: Sweden/Thailand

On 22 June 1995 the Stockholm District Court sentenced Boris Bjorkmann, a 66-year-old Swedish citizen living in Stockholm, to three months' imprisonment for sexually abusing a 13-year-old Thai boy. He was convicted of actual and attempted sexual intercourse with a child aged under 15 years of age, in violation of Chapter 6(5) of the Swedish Criminal Code. The maximum sentence would have been four years. Bjorkmann had been arrested earlier in Thailand, accused of violating the Thai Criminal Code, Section 279, namely indecent acts against a child not over 15 years, whether or not the child consents. The maximum sentence in Thailand is ten years' imprisonment.

Swedish extraterritorial legislation has been in existence for 36 years, but until this case, it had been little implemented. It was largely due to NGO pressure that Bjorkmann was successfully prosecuted under the legislation, and it provides an example that, it is hoped, will deter potential future abusers of children.

This story is a mixture of Swedish–Thai cooperation on the one hand, and of misunderstanding on the other. The arrest of Bjorkmann was brought about as one of the first attempts to target foreign paedophiles in South Asia. Following a conference in Bangkok on 'Children in Prostitution: Victims of Tourism in Asia' held in March 1992, organized by the ECPAT International Campaign, Sudarat Sereewat-Srisang, the Thai executive secretary of ECPAT, spoke of the need to control both supply and demand in tackling the sexual abuse of children. Sweden responded positively to this suggestion, and agreed that Swedes going to Thailand for such purposes should be watched. Swedish police officers in Thailand were already fully occupied in the suppression of narcotics, so two more officers were sent to Thailand. They were off duty, and came ostensibly as tourists to observe Swedish paedophiles in Pattaya. The Swedish police were offered cooperation by their Thai counterparts in making any arrests.

One of the off-duty policemen approached and befriended Bjorkmann after observing his activities over a period of time. Bjorkmann assumed that the officer was also a paedophile, and he dropped his guard and spoke openly about his activities with children in Pattaya. In February 1993, he confided to his imagined paedophile friend that he was to have sex with a 14-year-old in his hotel room that same evening. The information was passed on to the Thai police, and that is how they came to arrest him.

Bjorkmann had been to Thailand and the Philippines several times, staying at seaside resorts such as Pattaya. He was known to associate with young boys. At the time of his arrest in Thailand, he was travelling alone, and had been in the country for about six weeks. Bjorkmann said he met Pong at a bar after a boxing match, and although Pong corroborated this, he amended his testimony afterwards, declaring that they had met on the beach. Having seen the boy boxing, Bjorkmann approached him in the company of a 19-year-old Thai called Mr Guy. Mr Guy asked the boy if he wanted to take a walk with a *falang*, or Westerner. In his testimony, the boy said he had no idea how the walk would end.

Pong went with Bjorkmann and Mr Guy, but was later left alone with the Swede in his room in the Jamtiem Hotel. Bjorkmann said he would like to take some photographs of Pong, and agreed to pay him 400 baht (US$16). Although his testimony on this point is not clear, it seems that Pong agreed to this because he had no money. In the hotel room Bjorkmann kissed Pong and told him to take his clothes off to have a bath. When the boy came out of the bathroom, Bjorkmann was naked. The two spent the night together, and Bjorkmann abused Pong, even though the boy tried to escape. He told Pong to masturbate him. The following morning, Bjorkmann gave Pong 400 baht. He also paid for a visit by Pong to the doctor, since he had injured his right under-arm during a boxing match. Bjorkmann did take photographs of Pong, both on the beach and in the hotel room. They were not really pornographic pictures – Pong was always wearing underpants. Pong agreed to meet Bjorkmann again in two weeks' time.

Their second meeting was a repetition of the first, with a repeat of the abuse, and a payment of 400 baht. Later, the two met by chance in the Chai Ling bar. Pong claimed that when Bjorkmann asked if he wanted to go with him on this occasion, he refused. Bjorkmann, however, took him by the hand, and they went to the hotel room. After taking a shower, they went to bed together, but before any contact took place, there was a knock at the door. When Bjorkmann opened it, the Thai police rushed into the room, where they saw him naked with the boy. The police found several photographs of various Thai boys between the ages of about 12 and 14, with whom he may have had sexual relations, but none of these boys could be identified or located. Bjorkmann and Pong were taken together in the same car to the police station and placed in adjacent cells. Bjorkmann was later transferred to the prison in Chon Buri.

Pong was questioned by armed police at the station. It was for him a very frightening experience, and he admitted that the story he told them differed somewhat from the information he later gave before the Stockholm City Court. The police at Pattaya were not sensitive towards Pong, and were untrained in dealing with victims of abuse. After three nights in prison, Pong was taken to the remand centre in Tjonbole, and from there to the prison in Pattaya. Two days later, he was taken to an orphanage, where he stayed for one week before he ran away. Eventually, he found his way back home to his family in Khon Kaen province. Pong gave a second statement in September 1994 in the presence of a new Thai police investigator, a Thai prosecutor and the Swedish team, which was made up of a prosecutor, two police officials and a defence lawyer. This interview was conducted in a more child-friendly way. Pong's statement was recorded by audio- and video-tape. At this time, he was 13 years old.

In spite of objections from the Thai police, on 5 March 1993 Bjorkmann was granted bail by the Thai Court on payment of a surety of 150,000 baht (US$6,000). The Thai authorities confiscated his passport and he was forbidden to leave the country. He was to appear again before the Court in two weeks' time. Bjorkmann, however, applied for a new passport, and as is required by Swedish law, was issued with one within a few hours. He escaped from Thailand and returned to Sweden. It later emerged later that immigration officials said they had no power to prevent Bjorkmann from leaving the country, since this condition was not set by the judge when he granted bail. On his return, he was not arrested immediately, but was warned by the Swedish prosecutor that he might be at risk of extradition to Thailand if he visited other countries that might be willing to do this. Extradition from Sweden was not possible, since there is no treaty between Thailand and Sweden.

There were considerable misunderstandings and subsequent recriminations between the Thai and Swedish authorities. The Thai police and an adviser to the former prime minister expressed their puzzlement over why Bjorkmann's escape was facilitated by the Swedish Embassy. The Swedish authorities found it difficult to understand why Bjorkmann had been released on bail in the first place. Bjorkmann obtained his new passport before the order to arrest him had come to the notice of Embassy staff. The Embassy incurred further criticism, since its personnel lent Bjorkmann a car and accompanied him to the Immigration Division and to the police station, where he reported his passport lost. Later, the proceedings against Bjorkmann were delayed since all communication between Thai and Swedish authorities had to be conducted through diplomatic channels.

Following the escape of Bjorkmann, ECPAT Thailand and Swedish Save the Children worked together to press the prosecuting authorities in Sweden to initiate a case there. Altogether, it took a year of unofficial collaboration between NGOs before official coooperation was established.

The Swedish prosecuting counsel began an investigation into the affair in April 1993, within a few weeks of Bjorkmann's return. He was formally charged in April 1995, and he appeared before the District Court of Stockholm. The judge sits with three lay assessors. There is no jury in such cases. In keeping with the recommendation of the Swedish prosecutor, Pong, who was by then over 15 years old, travelled to Sweden for the court proceedings. These occurred in open court in Stockholm almost two and a half years after the arrest of the offender.

In assessing the reliability of the evidence, the question arose as to whether the Thai police investigation met the standards required by Swedish law. A second question-mark hung over the boy's age: the Court could convict only if it could be proved that Pong had been under 15 at the time of the abuse. Eventually, his birth certificate was produced in November 1993, with the help of ECPAT. It was not until ten months later that Swedish and Thai prosecutors questioned Pong, in the presence of Bjorkmann's lawyer, in the Swedish Embassy in Bangkok. This was recorded on video, so that it could be used in court. This time, the questioning was more relaxed, the atmosphere more child-friendly. Based on Bjorkmann's testimony to the Swedish police, the Court found that Bjorkmann knew that Pong was under 15 when the offence occurred.

Pong travelled to Sweden to give evidence, and remained in the country for five days. Swedish regulations do not permit children below the age of 15 to appear in court; by the time of the trial Pong was over 15. He was questioned in court for about two hours. He was accompanied by his lawyer, a female worker from ECPAT and the deputy attorney-general of Thailand. In Sweden he was well cared for. Although he did not confront Bjorkmann in the Court, Pong was asked whether the offender was present. He replied, 'Yes he is. It is Boris Bjorkmann who is sitting over there, but I do not quite recognize him, because now his face is full of hate.' It was noted that, unusually, the trial was not *in camera*, but open to the public. There was some discussion afterwards in the media over whether this would have happened had the child been Swedish rather than Thai.

Bjorkmann, who was unmarried, was the chief negotiator at the Swedish Agency for Government Employers, and lives at Bromma, about 7 kilometres north of Stockholm. According to his own deposition, he is homosexual, and has an interest in young boys in their early teens. He insisted that his interest in them was emotional and not purely sexual, and admitted that he enjoyed the company of joyful, vivacious and charming boys. In the preceding ten years or so, he had made frequent visits to Thailand and the Philippines. He said he liked swimming and sailing. According to Bjorkmann, he liked helping the poor children he met, and provided them with clothes, medical care and education. He described the street-children of Asia as 'fun, amusing, like little clowns'. He failed to recognize them as children, however, and persisted in calling them 'youngsters'. He liked to remain in control of the boys he picked up, always taking the initiative and rejecting those who habitually picked up *falangs*.

According to an article published by the sister of Bjorkmann in one of the leading newspapers in Sweden shortly after his arrest, he was a model citizen, who had been brought up in a religious home where the children had learned to distinguish between right and wrong. He liked beach-life and travelled to Thailand and other South-east Asian countries only to relax and spend time in the sun. She also emphasized Bjork-mann's love of children, and claimed that this was evidence of his innocence. He was also well known for his interest in children among the people in the village where he had a summer cottage. He used to arrange activities for the children of the neighbourhood and they appeared to like him.

Pong was thirteen and a half at the time of the offence. He was born in a rural area in Chumpae district, in the province of Khon Kaen in the north-east – and impoverished – part of Thailand, about 550 kilometres from Bangkok. He finished Grade 6 in a local primary school, and then 'went to work as an amateur boxer at Pattaya'. He had apparently left home with a friend so that he could train to become a boxer, and was staying with the sister of this friend who lived in Pattaya.

The family are poor farmers. Pong was the second son of a number of children, whose mother had two husbands. His mother and father were his legal guardians. In spite of his schooling to Grade 6, Pong could not read or write properly. When he left school, he helped his father earn a living by producing charcoal, which he sold in the district market. Pong's mother sold locally grown vegetables, which were collected from the forest and brought by other vendors to the market. The total income of the family was low, and they could hardly survive. Pong often had to find other ways of making money. One of these was to climb to pick coconuts from very tall palm-trees, for which he earned 10 baht per tree (about 40 US cents). Twice he fell from a considerable height and was badly injured; on one occasion his body and arm were pierced by a wooden stick. The family house was a small decayed structure on a piece of land belonging to a relative of his parents. Four people lived there: the mother and father, Pong and his sister, who, although a year younger, could read and write better than her brother. Pong's father was an alcoholic, and was frequently drunk. He often beat his wife, and Pong sometimes fought with him in defence of his mother. The relationship with the father was not good, and the situation placed a lot of pressure on him.

Although in this case the victim was taken to Sweden to give evidence in the trial of Bjorkmann, no proper treatment was provided for him, either in Thailand or in Sweden. In Sweden, children who have been sexually abused have the right to rehabilitation, for which the social services are responsible. In this case, there was no possibility of rehabilitation in Sweden, since Pong was in the country for only one week. It has been reported that Pong has had great difficulty in re-adapting to life in Thailand, and has been 'in conflict with Thai law enforcers' since his return.

Since Bjorkmann had jumped bail and fled the county, there was no indictment in the Thai Court. The dossier was sent to the prosecutor, and the prosecution order and arrest warrant were duly issued by the Thai authorities. That this happened at all was essentially due to the cooperation between Radda Barnen (Swedish Save the Children) and Sudarat Sereewat-Srisang of ECPAT, in pursuing the case with the Swedish prosecutor to encourage the Swedish authorities to make use of the extraterritorial law. Once more, the energy of NGOs was crucial in determining whether or not this offender would be brought to account. Sudarat subsequently left ECPAT, which is essentially involved with campaigning, and formed FACE, which is concerned with more active involvement in pursuit of individuals involved in child abuse cases. She helped collect evidence required by the Swedish authorities – the boy's birth certificate, for instance. She also liaised between Thai and Swedish officials for the investigation in Thailand in September 1994, located the victim and brought him to Bangkok for the investigation. ECPAT arranged for the travel and accommodation of Pong when he travelled to Sweden for the trial.

This was the first and pioneering landmark case in enforcing extra-territorial law using international cooperation to gather evidence. Before this case, some countries had extraterritorial laws that enabled them to prosecute child sexual abusers in foreign countries; but many refused to enact such legislation, under the pretext that it was unenforceable. This was the case with the United Kingdom, which did belatedly pass a law in 1997, thanks again to pressure brought by ECPAT UK and other concerned NGOs.

Media attention in Sweden was considerable at the time of Bjork-mann's arrest. Later, there were interviews with personnel from the Embassy after he had been issued with a new passport. At the time of the arrest, two people commissioned by Swedish Save the Children were present in Pattaya. Their task was to look into Thai law and to document the reality of its implementation in the area of sexual offences against children. This intensified media coverage, and probably contributed to the investigation set in train by the Swedish authorities with a view to implementing Sweden's extraterritorial legislation. Because of the intense media coverage in Sweden, the response it provoked was described as a 'moral agitation'. It was generally referred to as 'the paedophile trial'.

In many ways, the Bjorkmann incident became a test case, since it was the first time a Swedish national had been prosecuted for an extra-territorial sexual offence. It was certainly the first time that a victim of such a crime had travelled to testify, as a result of cooperation between the two countries concerned. At the time of the investigation, the offence in Sweden was classified as 'sexual intercourse with a child'. While the investigation was still going on, this was changed to 'sexual exploitation of a child'. The same sentence applies – imprisonment up to a maximum of four years. The earlier description of the offence indicated consent, which cannot be the case where a child is involved.

Since this case, legislation in Thailand was also modified. The Prevention and Suppression of Prostitution Act was passed in 1996 – a measure that had been pending before parliament for ten years. Amendments currently under consideration will have special regard for the testimony of children living on the streets. A working group, consisting of government authorities and NGOs (including members of FACE), has been set up to propose changes in procedure in dealing with cases of child abuse.

The role of the Swedish Embassy remains highly questionable. It was said that an Embassy official played a significant role in helping Bjorkman to escape from Thailand. The Embassy provided a new passport, even though it was known that his passport was with the Pattaya police. The Embassy tried to conceal this fact from Sudarat Sereewat-Srisang. Although cooperation between the Thai and Swedish prosecutors was of a high order, securing evidence, translating documents and forwarding through diplomatic channels instead of by means of direct communication led to considerable delays.

Sudarat Sereewat-Srisang, now of the NGO FACE, located the father of the victim and arranged for him to make a request for compensation for damages from Bjorkmann. The victim was awarded 100,000 baht (US$4,000) from the offender. Counsel for the victim had sought US$11,250.

Bjorkmann has served his sentence. The principle of double jeopardy did not prevent a prosecution in Sweden, since Bjorkmann had fled Thai jurisdiction. In Thailand, the Criminal Code does not provide absolute exemption based on double jeopardy, but in practice the prosecutor generally uses discretion not to prosecute anyone on the principle of double jeopardy.

In Thailand, the period of limitation is 15 years from the time of the offence. In Sweden it is ten years from the date when the victim reaches the age of 15.

14

The Ambassador and the Street-Boys

Jonathan Hamilton: Australia/Cambodia

Late in 1994, a young boy spoke to a worker with an Australian NGO for street-children in Phnom Penh about sexual encounters with foreigners. Why he came forward is unclear, but he mentioned the involvement of Jonathan Hamilton, a former Australian ambassador. Hamilton was employed at that time by the Australian government as a consultant to the Cambodian Foreign Ministry. The worker referred the matter to and sought advice from World Vision Australia. The issue was also raised with an alliance of NGOs in Phnom Penh (Child Welfare Group). This group had been established by NGOs, who suspected that an organized network was operating in the city to provide foreigners with access to under-age boys. The group keeps suspected foreign paedophiles under surveillance, monitors their activities and keeps a record of allegations against them.

Information on Hamilton was collected and passed on to Operation Mandrake, an Australian intelligence section set up for the purpose of pursuing sexual offenders against children. The Australian police began an investigation into his activities in mid-1995. World Vision Australia and ECPAT Australia lobbied the minister for foreign affairs to inquire into the allegations. This investigation became part of a wider inquiry into allegations of paedophile activity among Australian diplomatic staff in Asia (code-named Operation Arizona), after a member of parliament made public allegations in June 1995 against Australian diplomats and senior officers who, it was claimed, were engaged in paedophile activities while they were officially representing the country overseas. The MP passed 16 names to the Australian Federal Police, among them that of Jonathan Hamilton. This caused considerable controversy. The then minister of foreign affairs commented that such claims should have been taken to the police and not made public in parliament. The opposition spokesman expressed surprise that the Australian Federal Police had taken statements from the boys involved in mid-1995, since by February of the following year no charges had been brought. Following the change of government in 1996, he called for an inquiry into the recurring allegations of paedophile activity among personnel in the Department of Foreign Affairs and Trade.

The police inquiry into Hamilton took place both in Australia and in Cambodia. Having ascertained background information about him, the investigating team travelled to Cambodia to interview all those involved. The Australian police had no liaison office in Cambodia. They established contacts there through the Australian Department of Foreign Affairs and Trade, and received unofficial help from one individual officer who was already in Cambodia, engaged in a review of the country's justice system.

In April 1996, the police charged the 51-year-old Hamilton with unlawful sexual contact, including both anal and oral penetration of two 14-year-old Khmer boys living on the streets of Phnom Penh. One incident occurred in the grounds of a temple, where Hamilton allegedly had sex with one boy under a bush. On another occasion, a 14-year-old boy took a shower with Hamilton at his home, and engaged in sexual acts with him and his Khmer driver.

Hamilton was the second person in Australia to be charged under the Crimes (Child Sex Tourism) Amendment Act 1994, Australia's extra-territorial legislation enacted to fight child sex tourism. The police claimed that he had violated clause 50BA, which states that 'A person must not, while outside Australia, engage in sexual intercourse with a person who is under 16.' Sexual intercourse is defined by the Act to include anal and vaginal intercourse by any part of the body of another person or by another person by an object, and it also includes oral sex. The Act applies to Australian citizens and residents, and the maximum sentence for offences under it is 17 years. Equivalent offences are recognized in Cambodia, and although a person who sexually abuses a minor (under 15 years of age) faces imprisonment of between 10 and 15 years, in practice, terms of imprisonment are generally shorter. This is exemplified by the case of Dr Gilbert Selby, with which the Hamilton case coincided, and with which it has some points in common.

Gilbert Selby, a British doctor, was arrested in June 1995 by Cambodian police in a crackdown on foreigners involved in paedophilia. It was suspected by the NGOs comprising the Child Welfare Group that there was at that time an organized network of foreign paedophiles in Phnom Penh. Selby was charged with sexual encounters with minors, a charge that was subsequently changed to the attempted rape of five teenage boys. On 24 October 1995, Selby was found guilty and sentenced to two years' imprisonment, 19 months of which were suspended. Selby served only one month in prison after the guilty verdict, since he had already served four months while waiting for the case to come to trial. The court case lasted for only one day. Selby had been practising medicine in Phnom Penh for a number of years. Five boys, aged between 14 and 15, told police that Selby solicited them, bathed with them at his home and then had anal intercourse with them. S.P., a Khmer pimp, was sentenced to one year in prison *in absentia* on charges of procuring children for prostitution, and of complicity with Selby. One of the boys in the Hamilton case gave evidence at the trial of Selby. The pimp allegedly also procured boys for Hamilton. As the Australian director of public prosecutions debated whether or not to lay charges against Hamilton, the boys and the NGOs sheltering them faced kidnapping, bomb and death threats from S.P., the pimp, and one of the boys was abducted at gunpoint. He later escaped. Although Hamilton was not implicated in these incidents, the delays in bringing charges against him were seen by NGOs as placing at risk the victims in the Hamilton case.

The offender was a diplomat by profession. He was the former Australian ambassador to Cambodia and the Philippines, and had held other senior postings in the Asia–Pacific region. At the time of the alleged offences, Hamilton was a paid Australian government adviser to the Foreign Ministry of Cambodia. He was divorced, well-educated, and was described as being of 'high socio-economic status'.

The victim (Number 1, as he is described in the report) is described as a 'street kid', involved in begging and petty crime. He had no formal education, and did not complete primary school, but is said to have a talent for languages. He is an orphan (in the Western sense, both parents being dead; see below). An Australian NGO worker became his guardian for the duration of the case. He was homeless at the time of the offences, and living on the streets of Phnom Penh.

The second boy (Number 2) is also described as a 'street kid', involved in begging and petty crime. In identical terms he is described as having had no formal education, and having failed to complete primary school, although 'Number 2' is said to have a talent for art. He is an orphan in Cambodian understanding, his father being dead, but his mother is alive and is his guardian. He was homeless when the offences occurred, living on the streets of Phnom Penh.

The Child Welfare Group, which is recognized by the Cambodian government as an advocate on child welfare issues, oversaw the welfare of the boys in the case. Contrary to the views of some NGOs on the advisability of the boys being present at the trial, they were nevertheless brought to Australia to give evidence to the Court by closed-circuit television, with interpreters in a separate room.

Hamilton was not arrested, but was subpoenaed to appear before the magistrate for a hearing. Committal proceedings took place before the Magistrates' Court in the Australian Capital Territory in November 1996. The purpose of this hearing was to determine whether the charge should be dismissed or whether the defendant should be committed to stand trial in a higher court before a judge and jury. The magistrate found that there was insufficient evidence to commit Hamilton, and the case was dismissed. Hamilton subsequently returned to Cambodia, where he is still a consultant to the government of Cambodia. It is not known whether he is still receiving a salary from the Australian government. Although the case was dropped, Hamilton was publicly humiliated and his career has been irreparably damaged.

The boys involved returned to Cambodia, where they received no official protection, counselling or follow-up. In Cambodia there is an almost complete absence of such services for children who have been victims of sexual abuse. The department responsible for such provision is the Ministry of Social, Labour and Veterans' Affairs, which is under-resourced, receiving only 3 per cent of the national budget. NGOs managed to place both boys in step-families. One of the boys has remained with the family who took him, and is considered to be living a stable life. The other boy is missing, and has presumably returned to the streets of Phnom Penh.

Because no Mutual Assistance Treaty exists between Australia and Cambodia, the police were prevented from collecting evidence in Cambodia, such as searching property to look for incriminating photographs or videos. Although the Cambodian police were kept fully informed of the investigation, they took no active part in it because of inadequate resources and lack of training.

The prosecution depended heavily upon the testimony of the two boys about their sexual relations with Hamilton. This was what the magistrate found to be unreliable. Four factors determined this. First, the Court system failed to take into account the fact that the boys had been transported abruptly into an alien environment. Having lived on the streets of Cambodia, they were suddenly on a flight to a foreign country, where they were placed in a five-star hotel. They arrived only two days before the court case began, and must have been extremely bewildered by an unfamiliar culture, confronted by foreign food, languages they didn't understand and utterly strange living arrangements. They were allowed to leave their hotel room only for court appearances, and were even denied visits from the Khmer-speaking Australian NGO worker who had taken care of them in Phnom Penh. In the Court, they were accompanied by a social worker and police officers, and were 'reasonably treated'. But they were carried to the Court in a closed van, and arrived in an underground car-park with automatic doors. They were also hounded by the media, since a great deal of publicity surrounded the case. Under these circumstances, it is scarcely surprising that they appeared confused in court.

Second – and this is really an extension of the above – the Court made no allowance for cultural differences, which only heightened the confusion of the children. Australia has an adversarial court system, in which precise answers are expected, and matters of fact are paramount. The boys could not provide such answers. They did not, for example, know the exact dates of their births, since Cambodian culture does not regard the birthdays of individuals as significant and makes no celebration of them. In the Australian context, this appeared strange, and may have been interpreted as unreliability on the part of witnesses who apparently could not even respond to such a straightforward question. The boys were also uncertain about the dates and times of the offences against them. They did not possess watches, and in any case, in Cambodia, the measurement of time does not have the same importance as it does to Australians. The Court received no briefing on the cultural misunderstandings that might have been expected, and made no concessions to a culture with which it was not familiar. It appears to have taken the view that as long as interpreters did their job properly in translating the words, the whole case would have proceeded as smoothly as if the boys were Australians.

Third, it was part of the defence strategy to imply that the boys were being paid to give evidence against Hamilton. The defence lawyer relied on media reports that had suggested that the boys were being paid by World Vision, when in fact that organization had simply been instrumental in passing on to them a contribution for food and accommodation provided as an allowance by the Australian police.

Finally, the credibility of the boys may have been impaired by the persistent reference to them by the defence as 'prostitutes' and 'street-children'.

The medical evidence that was produced to establish the age of the boys (X-rays) was accepted by the Court. An adult Khmer welfare worker from an NGO in Phnom Penh gave circumstantial evidence, which included details of how Hamilton had asked him to procure boys. He stated that he had heard many stories from other boys about Hamilton, and had seen him in the company of boys. Further evidence included Australian government documents seized in Canberra and Phnom Penh, which indicated the whereabouts of people involved in the case on certain dates. Evidence also came from the police, who had interviewed Hamilton and had also interviewed officers from the Australian Department of Foreign Affairs and Trade, aid organization workers and journalists. The accused stated that there had been a foreign conspiracy against him. He claimed that disaffected individuals with whom he had dealt while serving as a diplomat overseas had initiated the accusations.

There was another significant element in the defence: Hamilton insisted that he was being victimized for his homosexuality. He was represented by private lawyers, one of whom, Richard Refshauge, was a gay activist, with a background in lobbying and campaigning. With his activist experience, the report says, he was able to use the media effectively to portray Hamilton as victimized because of his homosexuality.

Hamilton was represented by private counsel, for whom he paid personally. After the acquittal, he was able to recover most of his legal fees from the Commonwealth. He was awarded US$40,000 of the US$60,000 he had sought.

There are no provisions in the Child Sex Tourism Act for compensation to be paid to victims. None was given or expected. It is worth noting that in Cambodia Gilbert, following his conviction, is providing compensation to his victims by paying for their education.

In the wake of this case, ECPAT Australia is lobbying the Department of the Attorney-General to adopt child-friendly judicial processes. The magistrate commented that no Australian child would have been cross-examined as vigorously as the boys from Cambodia were, and that the questioning of children under the Act should be reviewed. The Australian Federal Police spokesperson suggested that the Child Sex Tourism Act should be used only as a last resort, and that more resources should be made available to the police to help investigations in other countries. Prosecutions should occur where the offences have taken place, in view of the difficulties in bringing children to Australia to give evidence.

Although there is an Australian Embassy in Phnom Penh, the fact that the accused was the former ambassador, and continued to be based there, made it very difficult for the Embassy to play a significant part in the proceedings against him. The NGOs in this case acted independently of the Embassy.

In New South Wales, at the time of the allegations against and investigation into Hamilton, a Royal Commission was sitting, looking into police corruption in cases of paedophilia. Prominent individuals were being named as paedophiles. This created a certain hysteria, and accusations of a witch-hunt.

Media coverage was extensive both in Australia and Cambodia. Indeed, it became a major news story in Australia, since the accused was acknowledged to be an expert on Asia, and Australia had a significant part in the peace plans then being negotiated in Cambodia. The case turned out to be very divisive within Australia. Hamilton drew support from the gay community, and some people believed the media had generated a paedophile-panic.

15

Escape to Japan

Hsien Nayagoro: Japan/Thailand

In September 1996, Hsien Nayagoro, a 50-year-old businessman, was arrested in the Little Duck Hotel in Pattaya, a Thai beach resort. The arrest followed a period of surveillance of Nayagoro by the Thai tourist police, who had been informed that a Japanese at the hotel often had young boys with him. An 11-year-old boy was taken to the hotel by a Thai national, a Mr S. The police arrested this man as soon as he had delivered the boy to Nayagoro, a service for which he had been paid a few hundred baht. The Thai police found Nayagoro in a hotel room with the boy. Both were naked.

The child said that he had known Nayagoro for about one month. Nayagoro was in the habit of meeting him at his school and taking him out for meals. Until this day, Nayagoro had never made any indecent proposal to him. On this occasion, the child was persuaded to go to the cinema with Nayagoro, and was brought to his hotel room for that purpose. He was told by Nayagoro that they would wait for another Japanese friend to join them before going to the cinema. He was invited to take a shower while waiting. Nayagoro then made the boy perform manual and oral sexual acts for him. It was at this point that the police entered the hotel room. They took pictures, and seized, as further evidence, six condoms and two pieces of used toilet paper in the victim's hand.

The Thai authorities charged Nayagoro with violating article 279 of the Criminal Code, a provision that prohibits indecent acts upon a child under the age of 15, and under which the maximum punishment is ten years' imprisonment. This applies to all such cases, irrespective of the age of the victim. Nayagoro remained in police custody for only three days, after which he was released on police bail. The police had seven days in which to investigate and prepare the case before it was submitted to the prosecutor, after which time custody of the offender must be transferred to the court. The right to bail is in the hands of the police during this time. In the event, the police returned his passport to him, and he left Thailand for Japan before the week was up. The case of unlawful sexual contact in Thailand is also currently being investigated in Japan.

The offender subsequently claimed, in an interview in a Japanese newspaper, that his bail was formally set at 50,000 baht (about US$2,000). In fact, he paid the police a sum of 600,000 baht (about US$24,000) in return for the assistance they provided to him in leaving the country. Nayagoro also declared in an interview that he had been framed by the Thai police. He appears to have been acting alone; there is no record of any involvement in a network of abusers. Nothing is known about him other than that he is an unmarried businessman.

Unusually, in this case, more is known about the boy. His parents are originally from Udonthani in the north-east, but are now in Chonburi. He was in Grade 5 of his local primary school. He was the younger of two sons, and his brother finished Grade 6 of primary school a year earlier. The parents fish along the shore of northern Pattaya, and the family is described as stable. The boy suffered considerably as a result of the offence. On the night of the occurrence, when he was taken to the police station to give testimony, a television crew and many journalists were present. A great deal of publicity surrounded the arrest of Nayagoro, and the boy's identity was revealed by the press. This, together with the fact that he was seduced at school, caused him great distress. He had to leave the school and move to another area. He received no treatment, rehabilitation or counselling. The family moved to another part of Chonburi, and the boy was later sent to live with relatives in a distant part of the country, close to the border between Thailand and Cambodia.

After Nayagoro had fled the country, the Thai authorities issued a warrant for his arrest. This is unlikely to produce any result, since Japan does not extradite its nationals unless a treaty exists between Japan and the country involved. There is no such extradition treaty with Thailand. There were police liaison officers from Japan in Thailand, but their mandate is specifically in connection with narcotics offences. They played no role in the investigation of this case.

At an unofficial level, things moved more swiftly. At the end of 1996, shortly after the arrest of Nayagoro, an official of a Thai NGO, FACE, happened to be attending a seminar together with a Japanese member of parliament, Mrs Masako Owaki, who lent her support to those in Thailand who were seeking to get the absent Nayagoro arrested in his home country. One outcome of this initiative was that a group of lawyers from the Japanese NGO Lawyers for the Victims of Child Prostitution (LVCP) went to Thailand to look into the case. FACE helped them with their inquiries, and they were able to get the child concerned to sign a form agreeing to press charges against Nayagoro in Japan. On 27 February 1997, the formal complaint was filed by the lawyers in the name of the Thai boy to the Aichi Prefectural Police. This event provoked considerable media interest.

Nayagoro violated article 176 of the Japanese Criminal Code, which provides that 'a person, who by violence or threat, commits an indecent act with a male or female person of not less than 13 years of age, shall be punished with penal servitude for not less than six months nor more than seven years. The same shall apply to a person who commits an indecent act with a male or female person under 13 years of age.' The significance of the age threshold in article 176 is that 13 is the age of consent in Japan. The extraterritorial provision comes under article 3 of the Criminal Code, which states that 'this Code shall apply to a Japanese national who commits any of the following crimes outside the territory of Japan ... crimes specified in articles 176 to 179'. The maximum sentence in Japan would be seven years' imprisonment. It is not necessary for the offence to be a crime in the country in which it occurred (although it is). Under the Japanese Criminal Code, an offender judged in a foreign country can be tried and punished again in Japan for the same offence. If, however, an offender has served a sentence abroad, the penalty in Japan will usually be reduced or remitted.

The limitation period for bringing charges in Japan from the time when the offence was committed is five years. A complaint by the victim is also necessary, and this must be filed within six months of the offence. Prosecution is ultimately at the discretion of the public prosecutor, who will decide whether or not there is a case to answer.

After the complaint against Nayagoro, the Japanese police sent a formal request for legal assistance by way of the Ministry of Foreign Affairs in Thailand. The Office of the Thai Attorney-General ordered the Thai police to hand over the file. This was forwarded to Japan by the Thai Attorney-General's Office in November 1997. Thai law allows Thailand to give assistance in criminal matters to every country in the world, even without a treaty between them. It was under these arrangements that the Thai authorities transferred the dossier to Japan. However, a year later, Nayagoro still had not been arrested. The Japanese police claimed that they did not have sufficient evidence, and suggested that the boy be brought to Japan to make a statement. The responsibility for travel and accommodation would have to be borne by the NGO involved, LVCP. Indeed, LVCP had paid for their own visit to Thailand to gather information in this case. They also bore the expense of translation and interpretation. Similarly, FACE in Thailand gave financial help to the family of the victim when they were contacted in connection with the legal procedure.

After sustained pressure by LVCP and the Japanese affiliates to ECPAT, and in cooperation with the Child Abuse Prevention Network in the area where Nayagoro lives, the boy was taken to Japan by Wanchai, who works for FACE in Thailand. No representatives of the Japanese authorities went to Thailand, and neither did they bear the cost of the boy's visit. He reached Japan on 15 August 1999, and was interviewed by Japanese police and officials from the Prosecutor's Office until 20 August.

Those supporting the child were satisfied that he made his statement competently to the Japanese police, in spite of the unfamiliar environment and the differences in culture and language and judicial system. Although there were some discrepancies between the initial report to the Thai police and the deposition the boy made in Japan, his story was consistent and coherent. It was observed that some aspects of the proceedings were child-friendly, while others were not. Nayagoro was also interviewed once more by the police while the boy was in Japan, but has now denied the offence. The boy and Wanchai left Japan on 21 August. Nayagoro has still not been arrested.

Indeed, since 1996, there have been a total of four criminal petitions filed in Japan against Japanese nationals who are alleged to have committed sexual offences against children. No case has yet come to trial in Japan, even though a number of Japanese men have been arrested, prosecuted and convicted abroad, in the countries where the offences took place. There still appears to be a reluctance on the part of the Japanese authorities to take the initiative in such cases.

In Japan, a new bill was introduced into the Diet (legislative assembly) in May 1998 prohibiting the exploitation of children through prostitution and pornography. It has not yet been passed. Among the provisions of this bill, thanks once more to pressure from LVCP, is an extension of the time required between the offence being committed and the complaint being registered by the victim. The existing time-scale, of six months, makes it almost impossible for a child victim to make a complaint to foreign police.

16

The Case of the United Kingdom

The United Kingdom was one of the last countries in Europe to enact extraterritorial legislation, which it did only in 1996, under pressure from ECPAT and the Coalition on Child Prostitution and Tourism. The reason given for the delay by the then Conservative government was that such legislation would be difficult to implement.

Helen Veitch, campaign coordinator of ECPAT UK, has been involved from the beginning. A coalition of human rights and development charities came together in 1994, when the issue of children in sex tourism first came onto the agenda. A major omission in the legislation indemnified offenders who, if they could escape the jurisdiction of the countries in which they had committed the offences, could return home with impunity. In the words of Helen Veitch:

> We tried to pressure the government on the grounds that it was not fulfilling its commitment to the 1989 United Nations Convention on the Rights of the Child. The Government gave technical reasons for its failure to take action. They said if they allowed extraterritorial legislation to go ahead on this issue, it would open the floodgates, set all kinds of precedents. They also argued against it on the basis of cost. Bringing evidence and witnesses from different parts of the world would place a great strain on public resources, and so on.

The World Congress against the Sexual Exploitation of Children in Stockholm in 1996 was a defining moment. It was held at the time when the Dutroux case was taking place in Belgium. When revelations of networks of collusion and concealment within police and government came to light, media interest became intense, and governments could scarcely justify inaction. The British government sent representatives to the Congress, where, perhaps predictably, and not strictly truthfully, they declared that they were world leaders in the fight against the abuse of children abroad. But after the Stockholm meeting they did prepare legislation, which was passed by Parliament in March 1997 and came into force in September of that year. The first conviction was secured only in January 2000, and that case was quite unpredictable and not in line with expectations (see below).

ECPAT sought the views of the Association of Chief Police Officers on reasons for an absence of convictions in the UK before January 2000. Helen Veitch:

> It seems that they, too, are highly conscious of the cost generated by extraterritorial prosecutions. They are finding it easier to get convictions on the grounds of possession and distribution of child pornography. Cases where pornographic pictures have been confiscated do not show pictures of children who are obviously and unequivocally under-age. It is difficult to trace children in Third World countries, and it is also not easy to determine their age with any precision. Registration of birth is often unreliable or does not take place. Looking at the outcomes of such trials, the police seem to judge that sentences imposed in cases of possession of pornography turn out to be about the equivalent of what offenders might receive under the extraterritorial legislation. It is easier to secure a conviction using laws that have been tested, rather than embark upon costly and prolonged cases in which there is no guarantee of success. The British police also say that to date, they have received no request for assistance from any of the governments in South and South-east Asia where such offences might have occurred.

In any case, ECPAT never envisaged that there would be hundreds of cases under the new legislation. It was seen as a safety-net legislation. It is designed to stop offenders jumping bail or escaping from countries where they have been accused and finding a safe haven at home in the UK. It does not even necessarily target preferential abusers, but is designed to deter opportunistic offenders. ECPAT has had contact with certain offenders, particularly those who have overcome or suppressed their predilection, and they have testified that the only thing that would stop them is tight legislation.

The contrast between the UK and Australia is significant. There have been about ten successful convictions in Australia, probably because there has been a more effective public campaign in Australia than in the UK. In Britain, ECPAT has tried to organize a public awareness strategy, through posters at airports, leaflets, and the joint efforts of the Foreign

Office, the Customs and Excise Department and the Association of British Travel Agents. On the whole, the tourist industry has been unresponsive – it says it cannot target potential abusers. ECPAT believes that the travel industry should take some responsibility. The relative success in Australia resulted from a high-profile campaign, which led to a considerable number of tip-offs to the police from other travellers who had seen evidence of abuse during their trips. Helen Veitch says that if other travellers are aware that such behaviour is criminal, their vigilance may deter potential offenders. Crimestoppers – a campaign in the UK that encourages people to alert the police to crimes they become aware of – has had no calls in connection with child sex tourism.

A second obstacle to the pursuit of offenders is the British government's concern for dual criminality in any charges brought. Helen Veitch says that Britain is very territorial about its laws, unwilling to inflict them on others:

> We are not good at looking at law in terms of international rights. This may change with the Human Rights Act, which will come into force later in 2000. If every country in the world except the US has signed the UN Convention on the Rights of the Child, there must be some things that are globally accepted. There was one case in Nepal, where a British national had abused children. Since there is no law in Nepal specifically against the sexual molestation of children, this man had to be charged there under some strange law about causing a general nuisance to the public. The case fell. Australia doesn't have the dual criminality rule, and that is another reason why it has been able to prosecute people at home for what they have done abroad. Enacting legislation is one thing, but implementing it is, of course, another.

Helen Veitch feels that we, the British, in particular have not come to terms with this issue:

> We haven't yet looked deeply enough at our own ambiguities in relation to children. There are some demons here no one wants to look at. Until we do that, children are not going to win. No one ever asks children what they think about sex. They are, quite simply, not supposed to have any views on it, nor even knowledge about it. We keep up a kind of denial that makes it easier to make scapegoats of abusers as though that were an end of it. It isn't.

Perhaps there is also in the UK – and indeed, in the USA, where legislation permitting the prosecution of those who offend against children abroad has existed for a long time, but is rarely used – a scarcely conscious sense that the integrity of the people of our country should not be impugned by foreigners. It may be that an imperial legacy inhibits a recognition that British people do such things in their wanderings through the world. It was – and is still – widely believed (though perhaps not openly expressed) that we, in our former incarnation, bestowed upon many of these countries the benefit of our civilization. Older structures of feeling still run deep, in spite of obvious changes in the world and the dissolution of empire. An instinctive reluctance to acknowledge to the world that British nationals commit such crimes may still operate. Certainly the numbers prosecuted in other countries – in the Philippines, for example – suggest that it is not a lack of examples that has prevented the authorities in the UK from taking action.

Similarly, the United States projects itself as the bearer of civilized values in the contemporary world. To some degree, the USA has inherited the sense of superior humanity that once distinguished the British in their imperial progress. We have only to look at the way Americans express concern about their own nationals, when these meet with disaster abroad. There is clearly a differential sense of the nature and value of the human person when it comes to their own people and to the people of the developing world.

And it does not require any great research to see that the behaviour of both British and Americans abroad is not significantly different from that of the nationals of any other European country – examples of hooliganism, air rage, football violence, and disregard of the cultural values of the countries to which they go as tourists are not hard to find.

There is no evidence that the United Kingdom or United States shows any leniency with offenders against children in their home countries. Popular demonstrations in the UK against the offender Sidney Cook when he was released from prison became a serious embarrassment for the government. The notorious Fred and Rosemary West case was in the UK almost as great a national trauma as that of Dutroux in Belgium. The recent jailing of the pop star Gary Glitter for possession of child pornography led to his public disgrace. All this suggests little enough sympathy with child abuse, while in the United States offenders against children have scarcely been treated with tenderness, either by the courts or by the people.

It seems to come down to a desire to protect the perception by others of the behaviour of the British and Americans abroad. Whatever horrors they may be capable of at home, there seems to be a wish to preserve the reputation of their nationals when they leave home. Indeed, these elements are also present in the cases from other countries recorded in the book, particularly in the role of embassies and officials who facilitated the departure of suspects from foreign countries.

Confirmation that something of this attitude persists may be gained from an examination of the law itself in the UK. The extraterritorial element in the law governing offences against children is the second part of legislation introduced to set up a Register of Sex Offenders. This register is not concerned with abusers in the United Kingdom who go abroad. Helen Veitch says:

> If they were really concerned about travelling offenders, they would not have introduced legislation that ignores them. It seems to imply that our children are protected, so why bother about the children of the rest of the world? There is no provision for passing on to authorities abroad information on British sex offenders. It refers only to convicted offenders, who are required to give their name and address to the police on their release from prison. The period of registration depends upon the length of the sentence. If they move, they must pass on their new address within fourteen days of moving. If they go abroad, they are not required to provide an address – they can go abroad for fourteen days without registering their movements. Indeed, if they go abroad, all monitoring of their activities breaks down. Offenders who go overseas are not on the register here, and neither are those convicted abroad. To get these omissions rectified is the object of a continuing ECPAT campaign.

In 1996, Stuart Mayhew was the first Briton to be jailed in the Philippines for child abuse. He was sentenced to a period of up to 16 years in jail for abusing two brothers, aged eight and four. Mayhew had pleaded not guilty at the start of the trial, but subsequently refused to put forward any defence. He is reported to have said that only God knew if he was at fault or not. The Court was told by the victims that he molested them while boarding at their house. It was said that he used money to ingratiate himself with the family of the victims, 'whose disadvantaged economic situation makes them vulnerable to the manoeuvrings of the accused'. The Court ordered Mayhew to pay 100,000 pesos to each child (about US$4,000). He was to be deported after serving his sentence.

Later in the same year, a British travel agent was sentenced to 16 years for promoting child prostitution in the Philippines, after being trapped by an undercover campaigner with Christian Aid. Michael Clarke advertised £600 sex holidays in a brochure promising that clients would find an 'Adult Disney World'. Clarke, from Eastbourne, was secretly filmed offering to arrange child prostitutes, whom he referred to as 'chickens', to the Christian Aid worker who posed as a potential customer. *The Times* (12 October 1996) reported that his brochure promised 'a short Jeep ride into "Sin City" to a very special establishment, the OK Corral, where dozens of headstrong fillies are tethered!' Clients were invited to 'choose your mount'. He told clients he could arrange sex with girls as young as 12. 'You have to give her a nice time and treat her to, say, hamburger and chips, something she's probably never eaten before. Then she'll do what you ask her for.' His tours were in the area of Olongapo and Angeles City, places where the sex industry (including a significant component of child prostitutes) developed in the shadow of the US military base. (Indeed, the role of the military in pioneering certain areas of the world as sex resorts should not be overlooked. This is as true of Thailand, which had become a celebrated site for 'rest and relaxation' during the Vietnam war, as it is of the area around Olongapo.) At present, such offenders would not be required to register with the police when they are deported to Britain. ECPAT is seeking to remedy this.

The first case of a Briton convicted in the UK under the new legislation was a 64-year-old campsite owner who abused British children in France. Gerald Draper assaulted young girls at his Le Grand Motives (*sic*) campsite in Brittany during babysitting and entertainment sessions, telling his victims to keep quiet about 'their little secret'. The *Guardian* (22 January 2000) reported that when police arrested him in his Exeter home after complaints from parents, he told the officers that he had a psychic rapport with children. 'They are good enough for Jesus, they are good enough for me,' he said. Draper pleaded guilty to assaults on five girls between 5 and 12. A retired engineer, he bought the converted farm with his wife in 1993, and hoped to turn it into a nudist colony, the Court heard. When that venture failed, he built a campsite and promoted it in brochures as a family resort.

He was very selective about those he accepted, using a marker pen to highlight the ages of potential victims, and turning away families who would not be accompanied by young girl children. After winning the trust of the parents, he spent long hours playing with the children in the swimming pool, in a hedged enclosure, on swings and in surrounding woodland.

Draper was sentenced to three years in prison. The case is unusual, in that the assaults were upon British children abroad, and in Europe. No doubt the proximity to the United Kingdom and the fact that British children were involved made the case easier to pursue, and it was less costly than a case involving children from Thailand or the Philippines.

Conclusion

To Whom Do the Extraterritorial Laws Apply?

Who is affected by them? Although it normally applies to nationals, some countries have extended the scope of extraterritoral jurisdiction to offenders who live in the territory of the state (France and Belgium), or even to those passing through it (Belgium and Sweden). In the cases in this book, there was no non-national involved, apart from Langenscheidt, a German living in Switzerland, some of whose offences took place in the Czech Republic. He could not have been prosecuted in Switzerland for these offences, since he was not a Swiss national.

Which offences are covered? In Belgium, France, Germany, the Netherlands, Sweden and Switzerland, extraterritoriality applies to all serious offences committed abroad. In these countries, pimping, or inducing minors to prostitution, sexual assault on minors, with or without violence, threat or coercion (including rape, attacks on modesty, etc.) and corruption of minors all come under the extraterritorial laws. But even these do not cover all possible sexual abuse of children. In Sweden, 'casual sexual relations with someone under the age of 18 involving a promise of or actual compensation' is not considered a serious offence, and would therefore not be prosecuted. In Japan, certain offences against children may not be pursued extraterritorially – pimping and inducing minors to prostitution, for instance. Producing child pornography abroad could be prosecuted in Japan and Australia, but only on the grounds that this would be considered corruption of a minor. Making, distributing, importing or exporting materials involving child pornography would be liable to prosecution in most countries, but not in Australia. Possession of such material would not be covered by Swiss legislation.

What are double indemnity criteria? Most countries in these cases require that the offence should be recognized as such both where the crime was committed and in the home country of the offender (Sweden, Belgium, the Netherlands and Switzerland). Japan, Germany and Australia, however, do not demand this. Double criminality is required in France for misdemeanours, but this no longer applies to offences against children. Indeed, in no case was there any question that the crimes or the penalties incurred should be the same in any two countries. The prosecuting country had to establish only that the facts constituted an offence where it was committed – it did not have to be an identical offence. In the Swiss case of Berger, it was considered that double criminality existed, even though homosexual acts in Sri Lanka are considered criminal, whereas this is not true of Switzerland.

Are there other prior requirements? In France, pursuit of *délits* (misdemeanours) cannot take place without a complaint by the victim or a request from the foreign state concerned. In Belgium prosecution of either *délits* or *crimes* requires a prior complaint. In both countries, such complaints must be filed before the time-limit expires, but once the complaint has been made, the time-limit on prosecution does not stop running. Both these countries have now removed this condition from some offences against children. In Japan, the victim must file a complaint within six months of the offence: in the case of Nayagoro, NGOs in Thailand and Japan cooperated to ensure that the complaint was indeed made on behalf of the victim before six months had passed.

What are double jeopardy criteria? Double jeopardy means that an offender should not be punished twice for the same crime. The French offender, Thierry, who was convicted in Thailand, returned home: not having fully served his sentence in Thailand, he was open to prosecution in France. The Belgian authorities could not begin the prosecution of Boonen until proceedings in Thailand had concluded. Boonen also claimed that since he had spent three days in jail in Thailand, this constituted a sentence, and should operate in his favour in Belgium. The defence of van Engstraat claimed that he risked double jeopardy, because the file had not been formally transferred from the Philippines to the Netherlands. Waldvogel did not serve his sentence in Sri Lanka: rather than prosecute him again, the Swiss authorities have asked for the file to be sent from Sri Lanka with a formal request that he serve his sentence in Switzerland.

In Belgium, France, Germany, Switzerland, Sweden and the Netherlands, if a sentence has been imposed by a foreign jurisdiction, it must be completed, remitted or statute-barred before the principle of double jeopardy applies. If any part of a sentence has been served abroad, Belgium, Switzerland, Sweden and the Netherlands will take this into account. In Japan, by contrast, even a penalty discharged in a foreign country will not prevent prosecution in Japan. A further penalty for the same offence is possible. The principle of double jeopardy is acknowledged in Australia in the Crimes (Child Sex Tourism) Act of 1994, but does not indicate whether a sentence imposed abroad would have to be completed for the principle to apply. An Australian national would probably be extradited to complete a sentence, rather than be prosecuted again.

What are the differences in the age of protection of children? Variations in the age of protection create a number of difficulties: this is 13 in Japan, 14 in Germany, 15 in France and Sweden and 16 in Australia, Switzerland, the Netherlands and Belgium. This factor is relevant only if there is a double criminality requirement in the country where the prosecution takes place. Among the countries represented in this book, Belgium, the Netherlands, Sweden, Switzerland and France (for offences committed before 1994) would be included. For a prosecution to succeed in these countries, the authorities would have to ensure that the age of protection is not lower in the country where the offence was committed. In this sample it is 18 in the Philippines, 16 in Sri Lanka and 15 in the Czech Republic and Thailand.

Which law – national or foreign? In all the countries in question, apart from Sweden and Switzerland, the court applied its own law to the case. Swedish and Swiss courts apply whichever is the more lenient – their domestic or the foreign penalty. In the case of Berger, following a change in the law of Sri Lanka – which raised the penalty from two to 20 years – the Swiss court applied the Sri Lankan law to offences committed before 1995, and the Swiss law to subsequent cases. Because of the complexity and intricacy of the application of foreign law, Switzerland is now considering abandoning this option.

Is extradition possible? Belgium, France, Germany, Switzerland, Sweden and the Netherlands either prohibit or restrict the extradition of their nationals, although Japan and Australia have no objection to the procedure. Extradition usually takes place on the basis of a treaty or reciprocal arrangement.

Characteristics of Offenders

Profiles The ages of offenders ranged from the twenties to late sixties. Their social situation varied from unskilled low-income workers to the extremely affluent, including some who had powerful protectors in their communities. One thing emerges clearly – abusers may come from any section of society. It should perhaps also be borne in mind that even low-income workers in the West can find the means to visit poor countries in South Asia; only the very poorest would be excluded. Such possibilities are emphatically out of the reach of the vast majority of the people in the developing world.

The existence of 'paedophile rings' is part of the folklore around child abuse, and is at the root of much of the current anxiety in Europe. In only one case was there a clearly operating network, in the repelling revelations of the Draguignan case, and there was collusion between van Engstraat and Bleicher. Several other offenders could call upon friends to arrange bail and bribes to officials, which may or may not indicate informal networks.

Some offenders had previous convictions for sex offences in their own countries, and one had been under investigation at home before his offence abroad. There was no case of a female offender, but in one instance a woman (the grandmother of the 9-year-old Priscilla) 'sold' the victim to the offender. Women are sometimes complicit in abuse.

The offences In most cases the offender could have been, or was, prosecuted for more than one crime – among them, abuse of adult victims, possession or making of child pornography and drug trafficking. Some were also convicted for such crimes in their own countries. Indeed, Claessens was originally arrested for an offence committed in his native Belgium (possession of child pornography), not because of his offences against minors in Sri Lanka. All offences recorded here took place in Asia or Eastern Europe, although it is known that such crimes are widespread in other parts of the world – Brazil, the Caribbean, South Africa and Morocco, for example.

Characteristics of the Victims

Profiles Victims were both male and female, aged from 9 to 19. All were poor, many homeless. The victim of Nayagoro was one of the few to be in a functioning family, in the care of his parents and attending school. The abuse came to light mainly through the work of NGOs. Most were deprived of proper adult care or supervision, which was a factor in their seduction. Many were driven by circumstances to expose themselves to the injuries they endured, and often saw themselves as powerless and without rights. Not all cases involved commercial transactions, although many victims had received benefits from the abuser, which sometimes served to conceal the nature of the relationship.

Status Some children were criminalized by the state: in Sri Lanka the victims were prosecuted for offences under the stringent anti-homosexual laws. (These are still in force in the whole sub-continent, a legacy from the British colonial era.) In several instances, the victims were exposed to intrusive media attention, and the Khmer boys assaulted by the Australian Hamilton were subjected to abusive court procedures. In most cases, the child victims were regarded as mere witnesses in a criminal case, and the relative official unconcern about their fate is an issue that requires attention.

Consequences for the victims Some of the children vanished after the offender's arrest. In the Draguignan case, a child victim placed in a children's home ran away; the other had run away before the trial. In the Nayagoro case, the child was so traumatized by the publicity generated by the case that shame drove the family from their home; a Thai NGO gave money to permit the family to start a new life. The Filipino victims remain in care of an NGO institution. There was, in most cases, little or no provision for the future care of victims. Some returned to the streets; the fate of others is unknown.

Compensation for victims Financial compensation was awarded to the victims in four of the examples. In only one case was this because the victim had a lawyer appointed by the court to make a claim on his behalf – against Brijthuis in the Netherlands. One offender, the Swiss, Berger, agreed to pay compensation himself. In the Bjorkmann case in Sweden, compensation was paid in the currency of the victim's country. There are no criteria governing the measure of compensation, and there is no supervision of its payment. The question of compensation – particularly to impoverished foreign children abused sexually – is as yet not clearly laid down in terms of to whom, how, the amount or the purpose of such redress. Compensation should be mandatory and supervised.

The Inquiry

What was the starting point of the investigation? Most cases were initiated either by NGO interest or a complaint from an individual. In one instance, discovery of pornographic material was reported to the police. In two cases, there was a degree of NGO entrapment of the offender. Some abusers would probably not have been apprehended but for the zeal of NGOs. This raises the question of how appropriate it is for NGOs to pursue suspects. In the story of Boonen, a media report following NGO pressure was the crucial factor. Only the Netherlands and the Swiss police appear to have initiated an extraterritorial prosecution without any prompting by an NGO. In the van Engstraat case, an investigation began in the Netherlands following contact between the authorities of the Philippines and the Netherlands.

How was the investigation conducted? There is confusion and inconsistency in the conduct of a number of cases. Many of the people and agencies involved know little of the legal provisions, and less about how to deal with cases involving children. The passing of information across frontiers is even more haphazard. On the whole, informal contact between police forces was very effective. More formal channels were often cumbersome, and frequently delayed prosecutions. The most efficiently handled cases used a combination of official and unofficial channels (Maurer and Berger). Such efficiency was not matched by a second case also involving Switzerland and Sri Lanka (Pfister/Waldvogel). In one case, the use of a liaison officer system proved effective. As far as Thierry was concerned, no action was taken against the offender in France, despite a conviction in Thailand, and an expressed willingness by the Thai authorities to be of assistance. In the Draguignan affair, no French investigation took place in Romania, in spite of the fact that this was the home country of the victims.

The technical requirement that a victim must file a complaint would have failed in the case of Nayagoro, if a Japanese NGO had not done so on behalf of the Thai victim. A certain lack of political will is also detectable in some cases. What emerges clearly is that the best way to guarantee an investigation is media publicity.

Other bureaucratic obstacles delayed investigations. The authorities in Belgium refused to press ahead with the Boonen case until all the documents had been translated into French or Flemish. The German authorities (in the instance of Bleicher) made no use of evidence that was available from their Dutch and Filipino counterparts. On the other hand, the taking of statements from victims in Sri Lanka was speeded up by the Swiss prosecutor who brought an interpreter with him. In the Maurer case, the Swiss police took pains to obtain evidence even though the victims lived in the countryside, remote from their headquarters, where communications were difficult.

All the transnational inquiries were lengthy, cumbersome and expensive.

What are the periods of limitation? These vary from country to country. In the Netherlands, it depends upon the seriousness of the offence. In all three cases, it is twelve years from the age of majority of the children. In Germany, as in Belgium and France, it is from three to ten years (according to the seriousness of the offence) from the age of majority of the victims. Switzerland and Japan, by contrast, count from the time of the offence: ten years for Switzerland, five years for Japan.

What is the time-scale of the cases? The time-span from when the crime was committed to conviction or acquittal depended on a number of factors, especially upon the willingess of the offender to cooperate, and the degree of coordination between the authorities of different countries, and equally, between the authorities within a country. In most cases, the time-scale was longer than two years. No prosecution has yet taken place in the Nayagoro case, in spite of the fact that the abuser escaped Thailand in 1996, and a complaint was filed in February 1997 in Japan. The

Frenchman Thierry has not yet been prosecuted, in spite of a four-year time-lapse since his conviction in Thailand. Claessens has so far not been prosecuted in Belgium, although the offence occurred in 1996: one of the researchers into the case for this publication experienced a six-month delay before information was obtained from the relevant authorities.

How many were involved in other offences? In most cases, offenders were found to be in possession of child pornography, but the investigators rarely pursued inquiries into the identities of the victims of the pornography, unless these were the victims found with the offenders at the time of arrest.

The Trial

Did children have to be present at the trial? Most child victims were spared the ordeal of having to appear at the trial. Their statements, together with the photographs taken by abusers or police, were accepted by the court. Where victims did appear, there was no consistency in the way they were treated. In Sweden and Germany, the children had their own legal representatives and were treated with sensitivity. In Australia, by contrast, the child witnesses were treated without taking any account of their culture and of the disruption to their lives caused by the journey to Australia. The children in the Berger case and the Brijthuis case were interviewed by officers from Switzerland and the Netherlands respectively: although the evidence was taken in Sri Lanka, they were not unduly upset by the experience. Some Western police forces have offered training to their counterparts in Sri Lanka and the Philippines in techniques of questioning children.

What was the content of the defence? The age of the child was the most usual focus of the defence. In Draguignan, the offenders produced a birth certificate that showed one of the victims to be over 15: a medical examination proved the certificate to be false. The Swedish offender claimed he thought the child was over the age of consent, but the court rejected this, following testimony from a witness to whom the accused had admitted he knew the age of the victim. Van Schelling in the Netherlands claimed he did not know the age of the child, but the court considered that her appearance should have been sufficient to indicate that she was under age. Proof of age is vital if a prosecution is to succeed.

Some offenders, even when admitting guilt, sought to mitigate the charges. They made a number of claims, which also fit a pattern. Some protested that the victims had initiated the contact because they were selling their bodies. Others invoked the cultural values of the country where the offences were committed, declaring that these were not hostile to child sex. In the case of Boonen, the defence tried to use a technicality, namely the restricted scope of the 1995 provision (which covers 'attacks against modesty committed on a minor'), arguing that masturbation is an attack on modesty with the help of a minor, not upon a minor. In the cases of Bjorkmann in Sweden and Hamilton in Australia, the defence sought to portray the offenders as victims of a society suffering from hysteria over child abuse. All of this suggests that the national legislations against child sex tourism are imperfect and should be kept under constant review.

The need for child-friendly procedures is clearly shown by these cases. The courts generally protected the children from being abused by the system, but in Australia they were cross-examined as though they were adults. Where children were represented by a *parti civil*, or a court-appointed lawyer, the rights of children were acknowledged, but there was no consistent pattern in the way child victims were treated by the courts.

What is a *parti civil*?   Only France and Belgium raised the issue of the representation of the public interest by an NGO; in the Draguignan case, an NGO did indeed do so. Notional damages of one franc were awarded, because it could not show any personal damage arising from the case. It did not seek to represent the child victims. Conditions for an NGO to do this have been eased in France since the law of June 1998, since a victim's consent to such representation is no longer necessary. In the Boonen case, the NGO was rejected as representative of the public interest on a technicality (namely, that this is possible only in cases of child trafficking). It was also refused permission to claim compensation on behalf of the victim, since it had no signed mandate from him.

What was the nature of the evidence?   In most cases, there was pornographic or other physical evidence for the prosecution. The tendency of the offenders to record their activities has been noted earlier. Such evidence was always accepted by the courts. There were usually statements by the victims. Either the children were physically present and gave verbal evidence in court, or their statements were taken in the presence of prosecuting authorities from the country of the offender. In those cases where physical evidence was found in the country of the offender (pornography), or the offender admitted his guilt at the outset (France, the Netherlands, Belgium), it may be asked whether a conviction could have been obtained on that evidence alone. Was it really necessary to gather evidence in the country of the victim? In Draguignan, the court convicted on the admission of the offenders and of evidence gathered in France.

How severe were the sentences? In most successful prosecutions, the notion was rejected that sexual abuse was less serious when committed against foreign children rather than those of the abusers' own countries. In one case involving a commercial transaction (the Swiss Langenscheidt), the Czech judge considered that the fact that the accused was not the child's first 'client' constituted a mitigating circumstance. The relatively mild sentence of two and a half years was handed down on the grounds that it was a case of 'prostitution'.

For the most part, the penalties were more severe in the countries where the offences were committed: in the Philippines, life imprisonment, and even the death penalty, were available, whereas among the prosecuting countries only Australia could impose a maximum sentence as long as 17 years. No offender received a maximum sentence. The highest was in Draguignan, where one offender received 15 years and two received 10 years (reduced on appeal to 14 and 9). Van Engstraat in the Netherlands was ordered psychiatric treatment as an alternative to a higher sentence. Boonen in Belgium, in addition to a prison sentence, was banned from exercising his profession. Most of the Draguignan offenders were deprived of civic and civil rights for five years.

The Roles of Various Actors

What part did the media play? Most cases provoked high interest among the media, especially in the beginning. As the number of such prosecutions increases, such interest may be waning. Intrusive coverage in the Bleicher and Nayagoro cases exposed the identities of the child victims, and the reporting was accompanied by inappropriate images. It was, however, media reports in the cases of Maurer, Bjorkmann and Draguignan that led to the subsequent police investigation. The media certainly contributed to public awareness of the issues, and sometimes provoked a positive official response: in Belgium, proposals were made for removal of the double criminality requirement, and the Australian government set up an inquiry into child abuse by overseas diplomatic staff.

What of the role of NGOs? The role of the NGOs has proved ambivalent, although in general they were supportive of the victims. One NGO in the Philippines was an exception to this, since it exposed the victims to gratuitous and damaging publicity. In the case of Berger (Switzerland), three NGOs worked towards a prosecution, and protected the victims. A Thai NGO was instrumental in pressing the Belgian and Japanese authorities in two cases that might otherwise never have come to a prosecution. NGOs used their own funds in several instances to protect victims, both before and during the trials. In the Bjorkmann case, the NGO paid for the victim to travel from Thailand to Sweden, and the same NGO provided material help to the boy and his family in the Nayagoro case. As a result of the four Swiss prosecutions in this report, a formal agreement on cooperation has been drawn up between the police and NGOs.

The prominence of NGOs in many of these prosecutions raises the question of their role in them. Should they give publicity to the issues involved and raise money for campaigns, and how proper is it that they should take part in the pursuit and, indeed, entrapment of offenders? Is it in keeping with their purposes to pay for victims or witnesses to travel? What kind of support should they extend to victims?

How did the Embassies of the offenders react? The help extended by Embassies to the investigations varied considerably. Some responded positively, with translation, advice and support, while others caused delay and hindered the inquiries. Some even facilitated the escape of the offender from the country where the abuse had taken place. In no fewer than four cases, his passport was returned to him by the Embassy in question. In one case, Embassy staff were aware that the wrongdoer was giving false information to the visa authorities.

Did the officials involved do their jobs properly? Most officials fulfilled their function competently, some even with considerable dedication. In the Nayagoro case, however, it was suspected that Thai police accepted a bribe, by accepting from the offender a sum far in excess of the fixed bail; his passport was then returned to him and he left the country.

Recommendations

Towards Improvement in the Framing and Application of Extraterritorial Jurisdiction

Extraterritorial laws There is significant scope for improvement in the application of the existing legislation. Some of the recommendations below arise as a result of problems encountered in the study of these cases. Others emerge from our observations of the working of the legislation in practice. These recommendations are addressed principally to governments, and their Departments of Justice and Foreign Affairs. Some are directed to the bodies responsible for drawing up rules of court procedure. We would suggest that the recommendations on harmonizing legislation should be examined in the Council of Europe debates, and other intergovernmental organizations. The recommendation on international police cooperation is addressed to Interpol. There is one recommendation addressed to NGOs, and we suggest that it be studied by ECPAT International for the drawing up of guidelines for NGOs involved in these issues.

Extending the scope of application of the jurisdiction

To the persons to whom it applies Extraterritoriality should apply not only to the nationals but also to the habitual residents of a country, as is currently under consideration in Switzerland. As to foreigners passing through the national territory, as occurs in Belgium and Sweden, we support this, but only in so far as such an extension of the legislation abandons the double criminality criterion.

To the offences liable to prosecution All offences of sexual exploitation and sexual abuse of children committed abroad should be liable to prosecution extraterritorially (as described in article 34 of the UN Convention on the Rights of the Child). Those countries that have laws that permit extraterritorial prosecution of specific offences (e.g. Belgium) should enlarge the scope of offences. We suggest that the following offences should be covered:

- pimping/inducing minors into prostitution;
- sexual assault on minors, with or without violence, threat or coercion (including rape, battery, attacks on modesty etc.);
- corruption of minors; and
- child pornography (including the making, distribution, possession, import or export of such material).

To the age of the victim The age limit for the protection of children against sexual exploitation and abuse should be harmonized internationally and raised to 18, which is the age of protection in the Convention. This age should be respected as the age of protection in all jurisdictions, since a person who has not reached the age of majority cannot give informed consent. Belgium is now considering raising the age of protection to 18 for commercial sexual exploitation.

Facilitating prosecution There should be no preconditions impeding extraterritorial prosecution. Territorial considerations are no longer consistent with the universal obligations to protect children and international concern for their protection. Conditions which might be eased are:

Double criminality A study of these cases suggests a trend to abandon the requirement of double criminality. This is increasingly at odds with international legal norms established by the almost universal ratification of the UN Convention on the Rights of the Child. All countries that have ratified the Convention share responsibility for the world's children, so that the prosecution of sex offenders against children is no longer a question of protecting the interests of another country, but rather a question of fulfilling an international duty to persons unable to protect themselves. Failure to prosecute suggests a country gives priority to protection of its nationals; this amounts to, at best, misplaced solidarity, at worst, racism. A second argument for abandoning double criminality is that it encourages abusers to seek out countries in which legal protection of children is weak. It is suggested that there should be an international statute that will abolish the double criminality requirement, and unambiguously prioritize the protection of children over the interests of nationals. Belgium and Switzerland are currently considering the removal of the double criminality requirement.

Prior complaint by or on behalf of a victim, or request from the foreign authority The need for a formal complaint is an obstacle to efficiency. Apart from the delay caused, it may lead to the failure of a prosecution, especially if the officials of the country where the offence occurred know little of the requirements of the country of the offender. In any case, a prior complaint is not relevant to inquiries into offences against children. We suggest that these conditions could be done away with by all countries, and with retrospective effect for offences already committed. The retrospective aspect should be no problem, since it concerns only a procedural matter, and has no influence on the substance of the offence.

Double jeopardy This rule – of basic fairness – prevents an offender from being tried more than once for the same crime. This principle should be applied in these cases only if the person was acquitted, or the sentence was fully served, or suspended. States should ensure that they do not permit offenders to escape prosecution on account of short-term detention or the partial serving of a sentence abroad.

Time limitation Time limits on the prosecution of offences against children should be harmonized, so that they run from the time the child reaches the age of majority. Any steps taken in a foreign country by the competent local authorities should stop time running in the extraterritorial legislation.

Discretion of the prosecutor A prosecutor who fails to prosecute in a case involving a child victim should be required to justify such a decision. It should also be possible in any country for a foreign victim, or a person or organization on his or her behalf, to initiate a prosecution, or to appeal against a decision not to prosecute, when the state authorities have decided not to do so.

Increase in sentencing options In all cases where sexual abuse of a child has occurred, the court should be able to impose psycho-social rehabilitative measures upon the person convicted. The court should be able to impose conditions upon his release, such as staying away from places frequented by children, and to impose limits on the activities he may pursue on release. Offenders could be banned from leaving their country of origin or residence, although this would be difficult to enforce in many countries. All previous convictions, including those overseas, should be recognized when sentence is imposed. The fact that a child may have been abused earlier, by another person, should not be a mitigating factor in sentencing.

Modification of legislation and of rules of procedure in dealing with foreign child victims

Proof of age This was an issue in many cases. Conditions for proving the age of a child should be relaxed: age should be determined by a variety of means, including medical and scientific opinion. The Australian Crimes (Child Sex Tourism) Amendment Act, 1994, may prove helpful in this context.

Development of child-friendly procedures Children should not have to leave their country of origin to give evidence. Evidence should be taken by video-link, or by statements taken (if necessary) in the presence of the prosecuting authorities and the legal representatives of the accused. If it is essential for children to travel abroad, they must be protected from media intrusion, aggressive cross-questioning and cultural shock.

Compensation for victims All child victims should be compensated. Claims for compensation brought before a criminal court at the point of prosecution would spare the victims further time and trauma. A fine, payable to the victim, could be imposed as part of the sentence; this could then offset any award by a civil court, should the victim also decide to sue. If an offender is acquitted on a technicality, the victim should still be able to make a claim in the civil courts – as occurred in several cases in this report. This is, however, a complex procedure, and inadvisable for foreign victims. This is because in a civil claim for compensation for personal injuries, damage has to be established fairly precisely. This is difficult in cases of child abuse, especially of prostituted children. A civil claim prolongs the trauma for the child, who may also have to submit to a medical examination.

The issue of compensation should be rationalized and administered competently. The criteria should include the needs of the victim, the availability of a responsible person or an NGO to handle the money, the possibility in his or her own country of rehabilitation and re-insertion into society, the seriousness of the offence, the responsibility of the offender for the damage caused, etc.

Psychological assistance and rehabilitation measures Such measures should automatically be ordered by the courts, even though the victims remain in, or will return to, their own country. Monetary compensation could be applied for this purpose in the victim's country.

Parti civil The civil law concept of *parti civil* should be enhanced for extraterritorial prosecutions. NGOs should be empowered to represent the interests of a foreign victim, as well as the public interest, especially where a child has no responsible parent or guardian, or where that parent or guardian is incapable of safeguarding the child's interests. Representation for a child victim should be obligatory. This would ensure:

- that a claim for compensation would be made during the trial;
- that any court order would be enforced, since there would be someone to ensure this was done;
- that details provided about the circumstances of the child would be accurate; and
- that the judge would be made to understand the impact of the abuse on the victim.

Without delay It is important that the offence be brought to trial swiftly. Where a number of jurisdictions are involved, the sooner the evidence is assembled, the greater the chance of a successful prosecution.

The need for enhanced expertise in extraterritorial jurisdiction
Information and training of all personnel involved in such cases

- Law enforcers: the application of extraterritorial legislation is a highly technical issue. Every country has its own rules about and perceptions of how things should be done. The jurisdiction is available only for specific offences, and may apply differently under different legislative provisions. Even within the same country, most law enforcers are unclear about how it works. The problem for enforcers in dealing with their counterparts in other countries is even more complicated. Several government departments within each country will be involved.

The importance of reliable information is crucial. Training of professionals – including lawyers, judges, prosecutors and the police – is an urgent priority in an understanding of the meaning of extraterritorial jurisdiction and how it works in their country. Specialization among prosecutors and police officers should be encouraged. Awareness of the responsibilities of states towards the children of other countries under the UN Convention on the Rights of the Child is indispensable.

- Embassy personnel: while most countries naturally extend assistance to their nationals abroad, it appears that some embassy staff fail to realize the seriousness of offences against children. Embassy personnel should be given clear guidelines on the responsibility of all states that have ratified the UN Convention on the Rights of the Child to protect children from such abuse. They should also be familiar with procedures for supplying information to the relevant law enforcement officers in the home country, as well as the foreign country in which they serve. A passport confiscated from an offender should not be returned to him, nor a new one issued, without the consent of the local prosecuting authority.

- Relevant ministries: Ministries of Justice, Foreign Affairs, the Interior and Defence should publish guidelines for their employees on procedures for extraterritorial prosecutions.

- NGOs: NGOs concerned with providing information should themselves be well informed, and be in contact with the relevant government departments and with the police in their own countries. At the same time, they should encourage their counterparts in other countries to do likewise. NGOs should be able to supply the media with appropriate pictures and images. Clear direction and a code of conduct should be established for those NGOs that deal with the media, the police or child victims themselves.

Improvement of international cooperation It is essential to set up channels of communication between the police, prosecution authorities, justice authorities and diplomatic personnel. Law enforcers in particular should liaise to clarify their rules of evidence to one another. An international database, comprising legislation on sexual abuse, the relevant treaties (such as extradition or mutual assistance treaties), case law and contact persons with relevant expertise, would be a useful addition to the resources to combat offences against children. Without mutual assistance treaties, states have to rely upon each other's good will. Treaties allow for the taking of testimony of persons in the foreign state, and facilitate the provision of documents, records or evidence, as well as the serving of documents and the location of persons or evidence. Documents transferred under a treaty avoid the expense of translating highly technical language. Whether or not a mutual legal assistance treaty exists, governments should allow direct contact between the relevant personnel. National focal points for extraterritorial prosecutions should be identified. It has been objected that in some countries the existence of the death penalty is an obstacle to entering into mutual assistance arrangements with them. Treaties can, however, provide for restrictions on assistance.

Other Tools of International Law

Apart from technical suggestions on improving the effective application of extraterritorial legislation, the cases in this report led us to think in global terms, and to pose the question of what other tools might also be developed. Extraterritorial jurisdiction should be seen as being of secondary importance: the priority should be prosecution in the country where the offence is committed. Victims can more easily be located, witnesses and other evidence are available, and there are no language problems. Extraterritorial laws should be applied only if an offence remains unpunished when an offender has escaped the jurisdiction, or when the acts do not amount to a criminal offence in the country where they were committed. Other options might be the extradition of the offender, and the implementation in his country of sentences passed abroad.

Extradition   Certain countries – Belgium, France, Germany, the Netherlands, Switzerland and Sweden among them – seriously restrict the extradition of their nationals. In some countries such restrictions arise from constitutional provisions, and were clearly devised to prevent their nationals from being judged in a country whose culture might be different, and in whose system of justice they lacked confidence. The existence of draconian penalties, including death, in some countries, for offences that would be less severely dealt with at home, obviously inhibits the readiness to extradite their citizens. Such drastic consequences may, however, be avoided, without having to rely upon extraterritorial prosecution. Extradition treaties may exclude extradition when the consequences for the accused may be too severe.

Implementation of a foreign decision If an offender is convicted by a foreign tribunal, and escapes that country without serving the sentence, it should be possible for the sentence to be imposed in the country to which the offender fled. This would avoid the cumbersome necessity of starting a new procedure. This execution of a foreign decision already exists in private law (civil and commercial), and is known as *exequatur*: such a decision may be carried out if it fulfils such minimum requirements as respect of the rights of defence, regularity of the procedure according to the foreign law, and competence of the foreign court. This principle could be more widely extended to international criminal law (see the Schengen Agreement of June 1990). States should also accept the possibility that their courts might impose additional penalties on those convicted abroad (restrictions on the offender's activities and the exercise of his profession where this endangers children, psycho-social rehabilitative measures). Previous convictions overseas should also be recognized to determine whether or not an offender is a recidivist.

Some Reflections

The fact that these cases have been researched, documented and painstakingly brought to public attention testifies to the hard work, dedication and tenacity of those involved in the fight against child sex tourism. Since the legislation is very recent, the efforts to achieve transnational cooperation have often been audacious and improvised. It is perhaps only to be expected that the emphasis will be on the procedures in the cases in this book rather than on the wider context, and on the long-term fate of the victims. With the passage of time, and the establishing of a considerable experience in pursuing offenders against children in foreign countries, the deficiencies and shortcomings in the legislation and its application will no doubt be remedied.

A number of questions arise. First of all, how widespread is the practice of abusers travelling to countries where children may be less securely protected than they are in Western Europe? The 1996 report of the United Nations Special Rapporteur on the Sale of Children and Child Pornography estimated that about one million children in Asia are victims of the sex trade (UN Commission on Human Rights 1996: 7). Child prostitution was estimated in 1995 to be an industry worth US$5 billion globally (United Nations 1996: 13). The cases we have looked at demonstrate the difficulty in distinguishing between prostituted children and other children targeted by abusers, and of course, for legal purposes, it is correct that no distinction should be made. Certainly, some of the children in the cases were prostituted – Rita in the van Schelling case, Priscilla and Miranda in the van Engstraat case, the girls in the Langenscheidt case. In the Berger, Pfister and Waldvogel and Hamilton cases, they were simply poor children, some living in a fishing village, others on the streets.

There is no doubt that with the great increase in intercontinental travel, and its relative cheapness, the opportunity has arisen for far more people to seek to circumvent the law in their own society by visiting countries where they imagine – sometimes, until now, correctly – that they will be able to get away with it. This has become all the easier recently because of the Internet, whereby those who want sex with children have been able to communicate instantaneously with others in any part of the world. And although there are always far more indigenous abusers of children than foreigners in any country, the mobility of offenders against children ensures that the particular problem of travelling abusers will grow rather than diminish in the near future.

This is not to say that the number of abusers is necessarily rising. Sexual abuse of children has always existed, in all societies. What has happened is that there has been a great increase in the opportunities for offenders to express themselves, both in the anonymity of broken communities in the West and in the vast migrations currently taking place in the countries in the developing world. These have sent millions of people from the rural areas to squat in the mega-cities of Asia, Africa and Central and South America. In the presence of this great economic and social transformation, the use of extraterritorial legislation can clearly reach only a fraction of the actual cases. It can scarcely bring to justice all offenders – the expenditure of money and personnel would make this prohibitive. It is hoped that the existence of such laws will deter potential wrongdoers from undertaking their abusive journeys. And indeed, there is bound to be some deterrent effect, particularly on the opportunistic abuser, who has not necessarily gone to the Third World with that intention, but may be tempted because he is away from home, and discovers the availability of young women and men on the streets. It is unlikely to alter the actions of those who are animated by an apparently unstoppable urge to pursue their desires – the extreme cunning and ability to cover their tracks of some of the men in this book provide sufficient evidence that they will not easily be deflected from their purpose.

There may be a distinction to be made – although this can also hardly be expected to be recognized in the legislation – in the ill-defined (and perhaps undefinable) area where 'paedophilia' shades into a search for 'under-age sexual partners'. This latter is a theme which recurs in twentieth-century Western literature – Nabokov's *Lolita* and Thomas Mann's *Death in Venice* being perhaps the most celebrated examples.

Recent research into the creators of well-known books for children, among them Lewis Carroll (*Alice in Wonderland*) and J. M. Barrie (*Peter Pan*) has revealed that their own relationships with children were often tormented and highly suspect. This wider cultural preoccupation with adolescent sexuality is reflected in much of the pornography on the Internet, which promises access to 'schoolgirls', 'teenage sex', 'barely legal partners', 'twinks', etc.

Much Third World prostitution recruits young women (and men) who fall into these categories. Julia O'Connell Davidson, in her excellent study *Prostitution, Power and Freedom* (1998), interviewed many young women in the Caribbean. 'Catalina', from the Dominican Republic,

> started to prostitute at the age of fourteen to support herself and her alcoholic father. She is slightly built and stands only four foot seven inches tall. In relation to her adult male clients, she is physically powerless. Like many child prostitutes around the world, Catalina drinks heavily while she solicits, and by 1 a.m. (when sex tourists in the resort where she works tend to 'pick up' girls and women), she is usually visibly drunk. 'I like to drink,' she says, 'it helps me to forget everything.' As well as helping her to forget, however, to work in this condition leaves her even less in control of transactions with clients and even more vulnerable to violence than she otherwise would be. (1998: 81)

Elsewhere, Dr O'Connell Davidson states:

> There are two points to note about child prostitution in poorer countries. First, because most child prostitutes are postpubertal most clients are not technically paedophiles. Second, the social organisation of both child and adult prostitutes varies enormously in the countries which host sex tourists. Some are directly coerced into brothel prostitution where they endure conditions of virtual slavery, but many prostitute themselves independently. (At a UK conference on Child Sex Tourism 1996)

There is also, in the West, as in many cultures, general acceptance of a considerable age-gap in male–female relations: the younger woman is highly prized, and much macho fantasy (reflected clearly in pornography) is focused on sexual relationships with young women around or just below the age of consent. There is some evidence from the sample in this book that European courts are sensitive to the distinction between paedophilia and sex with under-age partners: this is suggested by the relatively short sentence handed down, for instance, to Boonen in

Belgium (one year, with six months to be served) in contrast to the five years in the Berger case. Having said this, the imbalance in the power between prostituted juveniles and their clients, or the children and their abusers, remains one of the most constant and repelling features in all the stories recorded here. The profession of prostituted children is no more an excuse for the offences than the offenders' claim that they were unaware of the age of their partners.

It is worth pausing to wonder how widespread is the existence of 'paedophile rings'. It is part of the popular lore that such people act in concert. The analogy with the witches' coven is apt. The Draguignan case is the only example here of a network of abusers who acted in collusion with one another. Rather than 'rings', with all the associations these suggest of highly organized groups, the reality is probably loose associations or friendships between paedophiles, who communicate in-formally, by word of mouth, about where to go to find children and about which countries are believed to be more 'relaxed' and which more vigilant. Many of the men operate alone, although, as the stories in this book testify, they often ingratiate themselves with families, and even whole communities (Berger, Brijthuis and Maurer illustrate this).

It should not be lost sight of that many offenders were themselves abused as children, particularly men who molest boys. Of course, the majority of abused children are girls, yet most abusers are male. There is clearly some discrepancy here, but of the cases in the book, it emerges from the fairly rudimentary information on the offenders that at least two of them – van Engstraat and Berger – had themselves been victims of abuse. Julia O'Connell Davidson states in her research, 'many (though not all) prostitutes have personal biographies which include various forms of sexual, physical and/or emotional abuse. This is true of both male and female prostitutes, and such histories often leave people psycho-logically ill-equipped to deploy the powers they do have to positive effect' (1998: 39). It may be that women who are abused as girls express as adults the damage inflicted upon them in a way that is different from men abused as boys; but there is no doubt that abuse has long-term and dangerous consequences.

This makes concern for the injured children all the more important. It is essential that child victims should receive adequate healing and counselling, if the damage to them is not to fester and grow, and find expression in harm to a new generation. If victims are swallowed up by the obscurity from which their abusers plucked them, the sympathy they gain today will swiftly turn into vengefulness if they become offenders in their turn. Of course, not all victims become abusers, but many abusers were themselves abused as children.

In this way, there are practical steps that may be taken that will at least diminish the kind of emotional and psychological trauma that will only turn today's wounded children into tomorrow's offenders. Adequate remedial treatment for children is extremely difficult in the circumstances in which many of them live – streets and slums are not settings that lend themselves readily to therapy. But unless the plight of the children is addressed with greater care, we are accepting the 'sexualized racism', as Julia O'Connell Davidson calls it, of the abusers themselves.

This brings us back to the extremes of inequality that are often determining factors in the coming together of both offender and victim. It is called supply and demand, and the supply of illicit goods and services is a growing one in the global economy, whether it is the traffic in women and children for prostitution, the trade in captive domestics, or the business of drugs, illegal arms, endangered species, ivory, diamonds and other prohibited substances.

Most offenders are male, although the observation has been made that women occasionally abet, give succour and even encourage abuse, often in the form of relatives (less frequently parents) of the child who see in her, or more rarely, in him, a source of income. In the Langenscheidt case, the Filipina woman, Minda, was offering her 12-year-old daughter for sale. Women do sometimes take part in the abuse, and occasionally may become involved as part of a *folie à deux* with an abusive male, as in the extreme case of Myra Hindley in the Moors murders of the 1960s in the north of England.

A further question hangs over the stories in this book. Why do more than two-thirds of the cases involve men abusing boys? The researchers and compilers of the dossier did not especially intend it that way. It was partly accidental, in that these have been cases that have come to light through the researches of ECPAT. It is perhaps the case that paedophiles find it easier to find boys than girls. It would be a mistake to conclude that gay men are more predatory than straight men. The great majority of sex tourists seeking children are heterosexual. Since most Western countries have been at pains to eliminate prejudice on the grounds of sexual orientation, it would be unfortunate indeed to contribute to antigay sentiment by stealth or by implication. Julia O'Connell Davidson, whose researches into sex tourism are among the most exhaustive conducted anywhere, says that 'most sex tourists are heterosexual men who are interested in young girls' (1998).

Siriporn Skrobanek, in her book *The Traffic in Women* (1998), has shown how many women, including many under-age girls, are trafficked, not only to the brothels of South Asia, but equally to Europe. In fact, this traffic is a highly organized, efficient industry. Many young girls from Burma, northern Thailand and the tribal areas of Thailand have gone to serve men in Europe and elsewhere. Chris Beyrer, in his work on sex, politics and AIDS in South-east Asia (1998), tells of Thai women found in sexual slavery in places as far apart as Sweden and California. Research also confirms that many of the women in the sex industry in Bangkok began work as children; indeed, they still do so. Although difficult to prove, anecdotal evidence from many parts of South-east Asia suggests that the fear of AIDS has led many clients to seek out younger girls whose virginity makes them a low-risk option, and of course, commands a higher price, which benefits those who control them.

It may be that men seeking girls go to different destinations from those in this study. Certainly Julia O'Connell Davidson found that male travellers to the Caribbean and Central America were overwhelmingly heterosexual. She has also shown that the informal sex industry, where girls and young women use the streets, beaches, bars, hotels and restaurants, is far bigger than the organized sex industry.

This perhaps gives a clue to the preponderance of boy victims in this book. *The Sex Sector*, edited by Lin Lean Lim (1998), describes the economic and social bases of prostitution in South-east Asia. Citing F. Bruce 1996 (International Catholic Child Bureau), it states:

> It has to be faced that not all children are forced by someone else into prostitution and that some sell themselves of their own accord, not because they want to, but because economic and social circumstances may dictate such a course of action (is this then voluntary?)

The passage goes on to state:

> Some surveys have revealed that while there is a high degree of coercion involved in the commercial sexual exploitation of girls, prostitution involving boys rarely tends to be coercive. Girls are sold and trafficked, incarcerated in brothels, raped, deceived and abused. Boys involved in

commercial sex, especially those involved in sex tourism, are more likely to do so as a matter of 'choice' or through peer pressure, and the links with clients are more casually made (e.g. on streets and beaches or in bars).

It is certainly true that those looking for sexual relations with male children in the sample here tended to operate in public spaces, malls, beaches, etc. Adolescent boys simply 'hang out' in shopping precincts, public parks and sportsgrounds, which means they are generally more accessible than girls. Many offenders against boys worked by gaining their sympathy, perhaps by offering them gifts, clothes, trips to the cinema and restaurant meals, by paying for holidays and education, and by insinuating themselves with parents in the guise of benefactors. This creates – or has created hitherto – less suspicion than a middle-aged male offering the same things to a girl. The respective roles of patron and client are culturally acknowledged as part of the social landscape of much of South and South-east Asia. These provide legitimate roles for men to assume in relation to boys, which simply do not exist when it comes to girls. The economic status of some offenders enables them to masquerade as philanthropists, as providers of employment. Berger, for instance, was a considerable employer of labour in the village in Sri Lanka. When stories about his activities began to circulate, counter-demonstrations in his favour were organized. This also gives a hint of how far economic necessity can induce people to set aside their customary moral values if there is some material advantage to them in doing so. This example also serves as a metaphor for other kinds of collusion, especially that where relatives or guardians of children take the side of their 'benefactor', even at their child's expense: even some of the parents of the children abused by Berger joined the ranks of those supporting him. If we add to the cultural opportunism in concealment of their real intentions the extraordinary vanity of many of the men in the sample here, their sense of invulnerability, their protestations of innocence when caught, we may gain some insight into their psyches.

Adult men seeking relationships with young girls must of necessity operate more furtively in such societies. Providing girls for foreigners is probably more highly organized, but also more secretive. T. Truong, in *Sex, Money and Morality* (1990), gives a glimpse of the confinement of child prostitutes in Bangkok brothels:

The working hours of the children depend on the places where they work, and can range from a full day to periods ranging between 6 and 13 hours. On average, they serve three customers a day, or maximally 12 to 15. Fresh and attractive children are paid between 50 and 150 baht per customer, of which the owner takes a share. Less fortunate children sold into indentureship get a 5 baht allowance per day or as little as 20 baht per week until the debt has been fully covered.

Truong is not necessarily referring to brothels that serve sex tourists, and the extent of such brothels specifically for foreigners remains unknown. This is an area that would benefit from greater research than it has so far received.

Certain countries have gained an unsought reputation as destinations for child sex tourists. Why Sri Lanka should have done so is unclear, but there is evidence that the use of military bases at Olongapo in the Philippines may have started the custom there, and the presence of US army personnel in Bangkok for 'rest and recreation' at the time of the Vietnam war certainly gave an international impetus to an already existing sex industry. But it is possible only to suggest intuitive reasons why this or that country should have seen a disproportionate number of offenders from the affluent West. Certainly, where an effort is made to co-ordinate legal procedures, it is essential that cultural differences should be looked at, since without this, the kind of misunderstandings and lack of cooperation exemplified in some of these cases will not be remedied. This is not to concede the point that many paedophiles make, that they behave as they do because the culture permits it (that can be no excuse for their behaviour), but to acknowledge that cultural differences do exist, and that these give rise to a number of misperceptions and cross-purposes between professionals who work in a variety of religious, moral and cultural traditions.

It is impossible not to return to the issue of the fate of the abused children. In the van Schelling case, a great deal of effort was made in tracing Rita, but where her subsequent fate is concerned, the details are sketchy. It should be stated that ECPAT and other NGOs campaigning against child sex tourism are not themselves child welfare organizations, although many have tried to ensure that the children are properly cared for after they have been abused. Some have maintained contact with child victims, and have been instrumental in ensuring that they receive appropriate help.

It is important that the extraterritorial legislation be seen as part of a more extensive armoury in the protection of children. They must not appear to be of interest simply in so far as they can be brought into court to convict abusive foreigners. To do so is to distort the issue, so that the moral supremacy of the West, the fact that the rich industrial countries demonstrate to the world that they will not tolerate offences committed by their citizens against children, becomes the point of these cases. Is the legislation intended to protect vulnerable children, or is its intention to send a moral signal to its own people and to the world? A balance has to be struck. It is all very well for Western authorities to declare piously that Rita – and all the rest of them – have no choice but to turn to prostitution, but where does responsibility lie, in an era of unchosen globalization, for such choicelessness? These are not idle questions, for they go to the heart of the matter, which is that of an *institutionalized abusiveness* that governs the relationship between rich and poor in the world.

A word should be said about compensation for victims. The payment of a considerable sum of money to children in compensation for damage caused by abusers exhibits a perhaps understandable but questionable Western reflex – our naive faith in the healing power of money. Sudden access to a lot of money as a consequence of abuse will certainly set the children apart from their peers. It is likely to turn them – even if only briefly – into privileged individuals in the slum neighbourhoods and settlements where they live. It may even come to be seen as the equivalent of winning the lottery – no one should underestimate the effects that such payments will have upon the recipients. It is unhelpful in the extreme to be sentimental about childhood in the cities of the Third World. The harm that has been done to them is psychological and emotional, and money is not, after all, a vehicle of redemption. The messages, both to them and to others in the places where they live, will almost certainly not be the ones that well-meaning givers of compensation anticipate. This is another area in which the social and economic context of the legal provisions requires scrutiny and the most careful monitoring. Provision should be made for education, possibly for work training, and certainly for treatment and healing. But the disbursement should be supervised and the settlement modest, certainly not in the form of cash sums to be handed over to victims or to families living on the streets.

There are, however, a number of good reasons why the pursuit of offenders should become the responsibility of their home countries. For one thing, the laws that prohibit such behaviour in many parts of the Third World are applied somewhat haphazardly. The maximum sentence for such crimes may be considered excessive in some countries – the death penalty for rape in the Philippines, for example. On the other hand, the ability of influential and well-to-do foreigners to buy their way out of their situation is all too familiar. The zeal of law enforcement authorities in the developing countries is also scarcely consistent, whether because of corruption or lack of resources, inadequate briefing of police and others – whatever the law in Thailand, for example, a number of bars operate in Bangkok and Pattaya where under-age children are more or less openly employed.

There is no doubt that the early success of many of the cases recorded here has raised public perception of the issue, and this may go some way to deterring other possible abusers. Too much faith in this would be misplaced, however: deterrence is of doubtful value, particularly when (as it almost certainly will) media interest in the novelty of such cases wears off. Offenders may well fall back into a sense of security that they can do as they wish with vulnerable poor children in the Third World. Child prostitution may have become a more secretive activity since publicity over foreign paedophiles threatened to damage the tourist industry in both the Philippines and Thailand. Government policies – tackling the problems of poverty in the impoverished north and north-east of Thailand, strengthening penalties against offenders – may have limited the more flagrant behaviour of both foreigners and of their own nationals; accurate information on what is happening on the ground is not easy to come by. The situation is fluid and dynamic. Abusers may already be learning greater discretion and they may also take precautions to anticipate and avoid detection. We have seen the deviousness many offenders deployed when they made contact with their victims – Berger and Maurer, for instance. Following the publicity generated by these cases, offenders may now put greater energy into concealment. It is essential to keep ahead of the offenders and be alert to the shifts in a constantly changing situation.

It is quite clear that many of the men in the cases in this book have felt themselves to be all-powerful and above the law. A considerable proportion not only try to justify what they have done ('I am only helping children and their families'), but sometimes exhibit an almost pathological pride in their own impunity. We can also detect a distinct racism in relation to their victims, visible in an extreme selfishness in the pursuit of their own gratification. The feelings of the children are not considered. Is this because they are perceived as lesser beings than children in their own country, or does it show that abusers are unable to perceive the vulnerability of those within their power? Or is it a mixture of both?

Other characteristics are shared by many of the offenders. It comes, perhaps, as a surprise that so many filmed their actions, made videos, took photographs of what they were doing to the children – van Schelling, van Engstraat, Brijthuis, Bleicher and others. Some even took the films to be developed in local pharmacies. It is difficult to know whether filming their abusive actions was intended to heighten their enjoyment or whether it was to be used as a pornographic stimulus for their own later use. Whatever the cause, the tendency to want to watch themselves repeat their activities suggests forms of obsessive behaviour that can only hint at the disorder within.

The role of the NGOs has been somewhat contentious in bringing the cases to light. It is true that without the pressure and constancy they have shown, many of them would simply have been lost in the labyrinths of international non-cooperation, diplomacy or indifference. There is no doubt that official agencies often feel threatened by the commitment of NGOs, particularly when these are undertaking work neglected by the institutions to which it is entrusted. But in certain cases they may have exceeded the limit of their competence, among them entrapment of victims and a trial by publicity sometimes in complicity with the media. Tensions do exist within the NGOs. Some see their remit as the pursuit of offenders, while others restrict their activities to campaigning and public education about the issues that arise. But the importance of their role in this issue cannot be exaggerated. As Siriporn Skrobanek suggests in *The Traffic in Women* (1998), NGOs also played a crucial role in bringing the problem of trafficking of women and children to international attention. On balance, their work has been positive and innovative, and, perhaps most crucially, has served to sharpen the response of the official agencies.

The question of extraterritoriality cannot be detached from what is going on within the countries that have seen fit to enact this legislation in the 1990s. Anxiety over the safety of children is high, and with good reason. But the concentration on sexual abuse, while a serious issue, has clearly also become a metaphor and an object of other fears. It is one of the few things that unite the vast majority of the population of the countries of Western Europe, as little else can do. Certainly, drugs, violence, other forms of crime – of which children are also often victims – fail to ignite public passions in the same way. It seems that here, at last, is something we can all agree upon – the sanctity of childhood, and its right to be free of sexual entanglements with adults.

But there is a contradiction here. At the same time, the insistence in the media – in entertainment, TV, pop videos, magazines, advertising – upon sex, its primordial importance in society, does not leave children untouched. The sexualizing of a whole society reaches deep into the psyche of children also. The fashion and clothing industry make their own contribution to the creation of images of adult sexuality among the very young. A report in the *Observer* (23 January 2000) drew attention to the increasing number of young teenage girls seeking plastic surgery, alterations to their facial features as well as breast enhancement or reduction. It is very difficult for parents to protect their children from the values of the market, including the use of sex to sell virtually everything. There is a vast pent-up reservoir of fear and anxiety about children and the defence of their childhood, and this seems to express itself in an explosive concern about sexual abuse. Liberals protest in vain that children are at far greater risk from automobile accidents, from mishaps in the home, school or street; they are also statistically at greater risk from members of the family and friends than from assaults by strangers: outsiders who intend harm to children become objects of uncontrollable rage and anger.

The same is also true of children in the Third World. If five million children die each year from avoidable diseases, if children are brutalized as soldiers in Sri Lanka and West Africa, if children of five and six years old labour in the sweatshops of Bangladesh, if hundreds of thousands are born HIV-positive, if street-children in Rio de Janeiro are murdered by those in the pay of businessmen as a kind of 'cleansing' of the city – remediable scandals of, arguably, greater magnitude than what we are dealing with here – all this nevertheless fails to evoke a response of equal shock and revulsion.

At least, we feel, we can actually do something about those who injure children. Bringing individual wrongdoers to justice satisfies a sense that we are not, after all, powerless in confronting the evils that stalk the world. Who, after all, can do anything about the great economic injustices that reduce the life expectancy of a child in Haiti or Mauritania to almost a half of that in Japan?

Yet there is a link between such issues, and it is important not to lose sight of it in the crusade against those who offend against children. It cannot be expressed too strongly that the vulnerability of children in the cities and villages and on the beaches of the Third World is occasioned by the same gross inequality that permits their tormentors to visit their countries and take advantage of their desperation. In other words, there is an organic connection beween the kind of privilege that enables abusers to travel, and the poverty that compels poor children onto the streets, and into prostitution. This is why the extra-territorial legislation is in itself not a panacea. It is not by making an example of offenders that the abuse of poor children will be eliminated. It is a useful and effective mechanism, and it signals the determination of Europe to come to grips with something which reflects so badly on its society. Its scope may be widened, its application certainly can be refined, its reach may be extended. That is a positive achievement. And to attain this, much effort, hard work and endurance have been necessary on the part of those NGOs and individuals who have succeeded in gaining recognition for one of the most ugly symptoms of a growing inequality that accompanies the – apparently unstoppable – force of globalization.

Everyone who wishes to do so can make a contribution to the elimination of child sex tourism. A list of groups and NGOs that welcome help and cooperation from the public follows. Tourists can remain on their guard, and report to the authorities anyone they observe behaving suspiciously in their hotel or guest-house or on the beach. Now that the issue is so clearly before us, we can no longer say we did not know, it is none of our business. The protection of children is the business of all of us.

Bibliography and References

Asia Watch and the Women's Rights Project (1993) *A Modern Form of Slavery: Trafficking of Burmese Women and Girls into Brothels in Thailand*, New York and London: Human Rights Watch.

Beyrer, Chris (1998) *War in the Blood: Sex, Politics and AIDS in Southeast Asia*, London: Zed Boooks.

Ennew, J. (1986) *The Sexual Exploitation of Children*, Cambridge: Polity Press.

Lin Lean Lim (ed.) (1998) *The Sex Sector*, Geneva: International Labour Office.

Muntarbhorn, Vinit (1996a) 'International perspectives and child prostitution in Asia', in US Department of Labor and Bureau of International Labor Affairs, *Forced Labor: The Prostitution of Children*, Washington, DC: United States Department of Labor and Bureau of International Labor Affairs.

— (1996b) *Sexual Exploitation of Children*, New York and Geneva: United Nations Centre for Human Rights.

O'Connell Davidson, Julia (1998) *Prostitution, Power and Freedom*, Cambridge: Polity Press.

Skrobanek, Siriporn (1998) *The Traffic in Women*, London: Zed Books.

Truong, T. (1990) *Sex, Money and Morality: Prostitution and Tourism in Southeast Asia*, London: Zed Books.

Addresses of Concerned Agencies

ECPAT International

328 Phaya Thai Road, Bangkok 10400, Thailand.
tel: + 662 215 3388; fax: + 662 215 8272
e-mail: ecpatbkk@ksc15.th.com

ECPAT Europe Law Enforcement Group

c/o Defence for Children International,
PO Box 75297, 1070 AG Amsterdam, the Netherlands.
tel: +31 20 420 3771; fax: +31 20 420 3832
e-mail: dcinl@wxs.nl

The full report, *Extraterritorial Legislation as a Tool to Combat Sexual Exploitation of Children*, a study of 15 cases, prepared by the ECPAT Europe Law Enforcement Group (ed. Sarah Alexander, Marja van de Pavert, Annemieke Wolthuis, 1999, 316 pages) can be ordered from the Defence for Children International office in Amsterdam for 28 Euro (postage and package inside Europe: 10 Euro, outside Europe: 20 Euro).

Focal Point on Sexual Exploitation of Children

c/o Defence for Children International, PO Box 88,
1211 Geneva 20, Switzerland.
tel: +41 22 740 4711; fax: +41 22 740 1145
e-mail: focalpoint-sexex@pingnet.ch
http://www.childhub.ch/dcifp/focalpoint.html

ECPAT UK

Thomas Clarkson House,
The Stableyard, Broomgrove Road, London SW9 9TL.
tel: + 44 20 7501 8927; fax: +44 20 7738 4110
e-mail: ecpatuk@antislavery.org

Index